LAUGHTER OF A SCOUNDREL

NICHOLAS GOROFF

CL<SH

Copyright © 2020 by Nicholas Goroff

Cover by Matthew Revert

matthewrevertdesign.com

CLASH Books

clashbooks.com

Email: clashmediabooks@gmail.com

All rights reserved.

No part of this book may be reproduced in any form or by any electronic or mechanical means, including information storage and retrieval systems, without written permission from the author, except for the use of brief quotations in a book review.

This book is dedicated to my grandfather Norman, whose work to better the world inspired the thinking behind these words.

To my father Alexander, a voracious reader whose reverence for writers drove me to become one myself.

And to my daughter Quinn, in the hopes that some simple verses of mine might, in some small way, make her world a little more thoughtful and befitting of her wonder.

I would much rather have men ask why I have no statue than why I have one.

— Marcus Porcius Cato

CONTENTS

Introduction by Justin Little aka Vernaculis — ix

The Problem Is People	1
The Real Radical Centrism	6
The Perils of Absolutism	13
The Absolutes of Peril	24
The Culture War Ruins Everything	36
Anti-Social Media	45
Cycles of Common Thought	50
Escaping The Echo Chamber	61
The Lost Virtue of Art	72
Comedy Gatekeepers	84
The Value of Writing	90
The Isolation of Writing	97
Pessimism	101
A Happy Sense of Nothing	109
The Solution is People	116
Acknowledgments	121
About the Author	123
Also by CLASH Books	125
WE PUT THE LIT IN LITERARY	127

INTRODUCTION BY JUSTIN LITTLE AKA VERNACULIS

Nicholas Goroff's writing is not a breath of fresh air so much as it is a sharp whiff of smelling salts for the apathetic and cynical political attitudes present in 21st Century America, or a slap across the face from a good friend who only has your best interests at heart. It doesn't matter how many "breaths of fresh air" one takes in if those gulps of oxygen are in the middle of an episode of hyperventilation, taken deep from within a coma of disassociation from one's society, or inhaled through gritted teeth bringing droplets of angry spittle along for the ride inside of the windpipe. It's become more and more difficult to self-reflect and think about developing situations due to the mass amount of distraction and information that permeates our everyday lives. Along with this is a gaggle of ideological loose-lipped political commentators that will let anything tumble from their mouths so long as it affects profit-margins in a positive way.

This collection provides some sorely needed space, even if said space is small, for clear and honest discussion. It's a needed reminder that essayists and commentators can still provide people with useful insight, and its mere existence is an argument against the fatalism of believing that we must accept our status handed down to us as mere consumers or potential ideological converts. After all, would we accept the work of a surgeon or engineer that works from an ideological standpoint as opposed to the reality they've encountered? Imagine if a surgeon believed that it was actually the heart that does the digesting because of a very convincing argument he read in Science Weekly. All of us would rightfully cackle at this man's incompetence as a surgeon, and yet we reluctantly grant political commentators this privilege due to their miring themselves in abstraction and theory whilst ignoring the physical manifestations of reality.

Laughter of a Scoundrel represents an understanding that all politics ultimately radiate from deep within the human condition, and one cannot separate the two when coming to conclusions about one's worldview. The political climate at present seems to be increasingly one of self-perpetuating outrage, and I think anyone being honest with themselves will recognize the blunted state of their critical faculties when they're angry. This outrage plague is not only represented by new media personalities, but by the New York Times which put the President's feud with the NFL on the front page and decided that airstrikes in Libya weren't important enough to warrant as much as a front page blurb. Goroff provides us with substantial arguments against an increasingly troubling "culture war" attitude that facilitates poor quality writing, art, journalism, and political commentary. He also laments the stunting of our social skills and the fragility of our personal relationships brought about via the age of social media.

All of the catalysts are present in America which would drive an entire population insane, yet Goroff has managed to avoid all of this, observe it from a lateral angle, and present a tough but caring rendition of our current mental state. The author is well-equipped to document and diagnose our reality as well, due to holding positions all the way from campaign operative to beer critic. He can dress up in his fancy vest and stroll around a high-class dinner party entertaining important guests with tales of mischief, or he can throw on a t-shirt and walk over to the nearby dive bar and cajole even the stingiest of patrons into buying him a round or two. Anyone who can navigate every single pocket of American life with complete ease must have a solid understanding of people, politics, and what makes life worth living.

His writing is reflective and technical, but not in a way that shies from harsh critique when it is necessary. He describes complex phenomena in a way that is easily related to. Many essayists find themselves trapped in a time-capsule from 1935, or doing away with all conventions whatsoever, but Goroff straddles this line quite gracefully by writing in precisely the manner in which he speaks. It doesn't feel so much like one is being lectured as much as one is being spoken to by an equal.

Despite the fact he will never admit this, Goroff is an idealist and optimist styling himself a realist. He longs for another renaissance of thought and art and sighs with grief at the state of our public conversation which seems to be restricted to surface-level political point scoring between a Left that will consistently "get the vapors" about any old thing, and a Right that has about as much intellectual heft as that kid in middle school holding a pencil not an inch from your face and mumbling with a mocking snarl, "I'm not touching you." The author cries desperately for a return of impartiality and for clarity of thought and speech. For politics to adopt the human element and mean more than "getting one over on the opposition." He desires a new wave of artists in it for the art, writers in it for the writing, journalists in it for the truth, and commentators and activists in it to make things better for their fellow citizens. Although in some cases things get so ridiculous and malformed that all one can do is savagely giggle at where we've found ourselves. Not with a nihilistic reverence for chaos, but with manic despair at the fact our possibilities are endless and yet we've chosen the paths that require the least amount of thinking. Either that, or paths that lead one to missing the point entirely. This collection seeks to overthrow every cliché that defines the political state of the 2010s.

So perhaps now when we see a pandering political con-artist, a disingenuous politician, another story about "backlash on social media," or the newest "hot take" from ideology peddlers, the laughter of a scoundrel will be heard echoing and bounding off the backs of our skulls.

THE PROBLEM IS PEOPLE

Our world seems often to be drowning perpetually in an ocean of serious problems. Economic stratification, environmental calamity, hunger, hate, persistent global warfare. These are all matters which everyone from prestigious academics and professionals down through the ordinary hum-drum work-a-day wage slave are aware of and to one extent or another, concerned over.

And of course, in their awareness and concern, each according to his ability, divines both sources and sometimes, solutions to these problems. But seldom it seems, do such reflections really serve as emblematic of the true sources of whatever troubles threaten the world around us. Sure, one can blame socio-economics or bad family dynamics for delinquency and crime. One can blame industrial interests and influences for war and corruption. Who could even blame them for doing so, as a cursory examination of such matters points, at least in part, to these being the sources of such troubles.

But what lies beneath those? What sort of governing dynamics are at play? What is the real source code for all the errors and failures that our program known as society seems to encounter?

The answer is as obvious as it is simple and cliché. People. People are the source of just about every major problem that people tend to encounter. It doesn't even necessarily need to be intentional most times. After all, we are relatively simple creatures. This becomes apparent once we allow ourselves to drop the façade of believing that simply because we can post pictures of our breakfast or car to Instagram, that we're substantially more evolved than a chimpanzee, or a pigeon, or a cockroach, or a strain of bacteria.

Christopher Hitchens often liked to say *"Evolution has meant that our prefrontal lobes are too small, our adrenal glands are too big, and our reproductive organs apparently designed by committee; a recipe which, alone or in combination, is very certain to lead to some unhappiness and disorder."*

When you consider the broader relative nature of the universe itself, wherein every concept imaginable from size and direction to morals and ethics take on natures that are relative to perception, the notion that we as a species are substantially or significantly "advanced" in some way only stands as true when comparing ourselves to creatures we deem as lesser. Even in this though, we're still forced to ignore how so many of the species we deem such are themselves perfectly suited to their environments in ways we seem unable to be or remain.

All in all, as imperfect and flawed a species as we are contrasted with all we've managed to achieve, the underlying source of nearly all of our problems ultimately comes back to us. Our selves. Again, a simple and cliché notion to be sure, but one which is also fundamentally true. Graft, corruption, predation...these are all matters usually rooted in greed and avarice, rage and fear and of course, natural human duality.

People often act surprised or aghast when someone references the handful of generally unspoken of kind or humanitarian acts of the now convicted "pharmabro" Martin Skrelli. The same people are often equally confounded when the malevolent, cruel and corrupt actions of Mother Theresa are raised in conversation. Though most anyone who thinks deeply enough on the nature of the human condition is forced to come to the understanding that within every human being equal potential for what we regard as goodness or evil exist. This simple dichotomy between a white collar crook and one of the world's most commonly revered humanitarians expresses one of the most dangerous underlying flaws to human thinking. That being; its eagerness to unquestioningly accept basic notions in the face of actual facts.

Should we be remotely surprised then that within a society built by a species which claims to value life and justice, that violence and horror are ordinary to the point of being mundane? Is it even marginally surprising then that as so many of us look back over our history, we dress it up with myths and legends that exalt the virtues we tend to favor while glossing over the often inconvenient realities and sometimes horrific complexities that went in to the original story? There is a reason we hear more about the steely eyed super-patriot that we like to pretend George Washington was, rather than the ambitious land grabbing real estate speculator and financial disaster he was in real life.

Delusion and myth are easier to digest than truth, for most. It allows us to view the world in starker terms of black and white, right and wrong, good and evil. But just as the intellectual short cuts that so many like to take make accepting the nature of the world easier, it also serves the inexorable purpose of allowing horror to go unchecked until it's too late. This ultimately, is one of the central mechanisms by which people, en masse, are the source of their own collective suffering.

Just as we manage to gloss over that which leaves us feeling uncomfortable without a sense of righteousness in our considerations of things, so too do so many bad actors in the world continue pushing forward their plans and actions, despite their often dire consequences, by justifying them in the augmented perspective of wishful thinking. The investment banking genius who creates a new system of generating private wealth while wreaking havoc on a broader economy, the politician who lets him do it, even the average guy on the street who imagines it's illegal immigrants who created whatever crisis which occurs... each of these people in their proper turn deploy the delusion of rightness as a means to justify or mythologize what happens.

When a nation goes to war over oil, fictions about defending freedom become the accepted lore. When an insurance company denies a patient treatment to save money, people accept it as the essential nature of the business. If a kid shoots up his school, everything from guns to video games becomes the suggested villain. But within each of these, the need for human delusion to reduce and simplify the matter into an easily digestible excuse for why such things happen becomes the norm.

And really, though it may sound harsh, judgmental or even nihilistic, it remains at the same time, a truth we can neither escape nor fully condemn. Beyond the simple fact that generally in our day to day lives we're all guilty of it in some way. This mechanism within the human mind is more a semi-primal survival instinct than anything else. How dismaying and depressing would it be to consistently acknowledge and dwell upon the fact that our ultimately simple nature is capable of providing the world with more justified evils than it can provide inexplicable good?

Yet fundamentally, people are the real problem. They're scared, flighty, combative and crude. Unlike the machines and fantasies we create to augment this world we live in, we're ultimately all simple, dirty mammals trying our best to survive. In this sense one could almost say that our intellects, the trait we praise the most while comparing ourselves to other species, while also being the source for our bitter machinations and endless justifications, is equally and simultaneously our greatest strength and greatest weakness.

Human duality. It's really quite the quandary. What is one to do when the source of their better nature is tied intrinsically to the blackened depths of their own selves which often go so unaddressed, they can become insidious monsters, capable of not only carrying out, but justifying nearly anything?

THE REAL RADICAL CENTRISM

There are times when everyone is wrong. Throughout the course of my life, I have been called many things. Personal pejoratives aside, the most frequent source of some sour maligning usually comes in reference to some dispute rooted in this or that political trifle. Taxation, guns, health care, whether a view is right wing or left and how definitively that view makes me and others of similar persuasions card carrying devotees of a given side, party or ideology. In a boundless cornucopia of bitter disagreement, there almost always seems ample room for one to lob a petty insult garbed in dress of an even pettier generalization.

However whether one has decided to call me a communist for voicing support for public services, or a fascist for not believing that the government itself ought to instruct us how to speak under threat of penalty or imprisonment, the single derisive dismissal I find most amusing is that of the *filthy centrist*.

It does truly seem that in an age where all are expected to have deeply held positions on all manner of topics, that while the effortless labeling of another as being one's own bitter enemy is in constant high fashion, deriding one for not being a sycophantic diehard is seen as equally effective in writing them and their perspectives off entirely. For my part however, I wouldn't have it any other way. So before I'm accused of being spineless and lacking in any and all conviction, let me clarify at the outset that to my mind, the only thing worse than having no concrete position at all is having one so deeply rooted in general sensibility that it's impossible to even dream of it budging one way or another.

This ultimately is because ideology itself is perhaps the most pernicious heap of tribalistic bullshit man has managed to devise since the advent of organized religion. One need not be an atheist to see the sorts of vulgar sycophantic philosophy and behavior that religious fundamentalism can breed. In the same spirit, one does not need to be a skeptical political centrist to see the same inherent to ideology.

From tyrannical despots seeking to establish global empires, down to the ordinary unhappy bastard who stews daily lamenting how the country is '*going to hell*' because of policies he may not like or understand, political ideology in many respects acts much like a religious orthodoxy, bringing out the absolute worst in masses of people nearly every time it can. In lieu of holy wars and crusades, the modern and prosperous west finds itself constantly playing host to a different form of crusade, wherein 'our side' is right, and 'their side' is evil.

This of course is hyperbole to a certain extent as not every ideologically aligned person is going to be driven into the arms of such pathetic reactionary movements such as Antifa or the Alt-right, but by sheer virtue of the numbers of those that are, a rather undeniable and wholly lamentable reality to zeitgeists, orthodoxies and ideologies is wholly apparent.

So where then does centrism fall in regards to what is an ever increasing polarization and radicalization in our political landscape? To put it simply and directly, above it. Not so much a position crammed into the middle ground of the frenzied bilateral madness of partisan fury and fervor, but instead a passionate dispassion and attempted objectivity applied as a discipline rather than mere belief (or lack thereof.)

I am of course generalizing in this context, however it is not a generalization that is without merit. The point once again being that while "centrism" is often derided and regarded as a meager absence of principles or convictions, to those more dedicated to objective reasoning than ideological point scoring, it is instead a means by which to attempt to become the tabula rasa of the philosopher John Locke. The blank slate in this sense, where rather than being encumbered by pointless presupposition one is empowered by a detached ability to look solely to objective reality at hand and draw conclusions from there.

This is not to say bias is rooted out entirely, as such is for most if not all people, an impossibility. As an approach to questions of political, social or even philosophical matters, the shedding of clumsy assumption in favor of rational impartiality leads to a broader overall consideration of the question or questions under consideration than the stale predictability of chattering absolutism. In effect, proper "centrism" is the catchall term for those who refuse to let ideology guide their thinking.

Consider now, a broader question of ideological orthodoxy versus objective reasoning in respect to the law. A standard point of contention in respect to the election of Presidents is their power to appoint justices to the Supreme Court. This contention and the ensuing battles over said jurist appointments seems to now routinely play themselves out not only in the Senate where proposed justices are confirmed or denied, but in the public discourse as well.

But how many average politically minded citizens have any real grounding in the practice and theory of law that extends beyond a DVD box set of Boston Legal? How often does the average political enthusiast, who themselves is undoubtedly brimming with positions and ideas about law and legislation, take the time to genuinely challenge their own perspectives, assumptions or beliefs? How many times in the course of however many Supreme Court nominations one may have seen over the course of their lifetime, has the discussion delved into the deeper and more nuanced aspects of law and judicial interpretation?

To be sure, while a great many on the political right like to identify themselves as "constitutionalists" or "constitutional constructionists," a cursory examination of what inspires them to root for or against a given nominee has more often to do with pop-partisan issues than actual judicial records or decisions. Take for an easy example the most recent fight –at least as of this book being written- over the appointment of Brett Kavanaugh by Donald Trump.

While I will openly say that I personally opposed his appointment, my opposition came after reading his actual judicial opinions on the matters of privacy, industrial regulation and his perspective on executive authority. To my mind, even if I am to admit an underlying bias in respect to my own long standing liberal sentiments, basing an opinion in regards to a jurist's judicial record is considerably better than the screeching bandwagons which tended to dominate the matter otherwise.

And here I am not merely lambasting the posturing or

presumed hysteria of an identitarian left who, without seeing any verifiable evidence of crimes beyond at one time being a boorish and spoiled fratboy chose to condemn Kavanaugh as a rapist or worse simply by virtue of mob thinking before even a shred of actual testimony had been offered, but also their opposition. From a framework of judicial consideration, neither side took to considering what the lifetime appointment of a man with a track record of flouting 4th amendment privacy rights in the name of security or offering paltry justifications for overarching executive privilege would mean for the nation. But rather from the same "side" from which opposition to the USA PATRIOT act itself first sprung, as well as from their opposition who root their political philosophy in an ostensible hostility to "big government," the conversation seemed to roundly ignore these matters almost entirely.

With many on the right or those describing themselves as right of center stepping forward to defend and support the appointment of Brett Kavanaugh openly on the sole grounds that it would "teach the left a lesson," the majority of public debate surrounding one of the most crucial positions in American government largely boiled down to a series of shouting matches between generally shallow zeitgeists.

Was it "rape culture" under Senate consideration? Was the fundamental purpose of promoting a permanent Supreme Court justice in such a way as many a Trump supporter did, an act put on to "own the libs?" To most observers looking to the public battles surrounding such, this is what it fundamentally came down to. Ask most strident armchair pundits from the rank and file left or right about where their support or opposition to the nominee came from and the citing of judicial decisions or penned opinions was not likely to be amongst their answers.

So here and in this we find what feels to be a void between opposing banalities without much of any genuine thought or objective sentiment focusing on what the end results of an appointment would actually be. The left hates what the right loves, the right loves what the left hates. This banter and bickering is endemic to the modern partisan structure to such a degree that in many cases the tribal animosity absolves itself of even the mere pretext of meaningful deliberation. Throughout it all, the forces and institutions which range in scope and power far beyond the often petty sniping that so many in the "arena" tend to view as meaningful conviction enjoy even lower levels of legitimate scrutiny and supervision, as attention itself is drawn hopelessly away from fundamental matters of import.

Just as the "violence" in gun violence is disregarded in the discussion of the matter, judicial decisions are sidelined in deliberations regarding a powerful judicial appointment, all in the name not of wise policy or sound decision making, but rather in typical fashion, aligned and supported by loyalists to given ideologies. Here, the baby goes out with the bathwater but inexplicably does so as a result of a disagreement about what to eat for dinner. It's inane, counterproductive and very often abjectly harmful.

While an objective rejection of presumption and orthodox thinking can liberate one's mind and perspective, allowing for the necessary clarity to truly understand a thing, the fact that such a rejection is unto itself viewed as abnormal amidst an ever maddening political environment makes objectivity and calm rational thought, radical acts unto themselves. One need not even come to the same conclusions as another who has also abandoned ideology for reasonable thought for such to remain a centrist act. But rather, in a time of boundless mob mentality and endless processions of virtue tests, the simple act of unsolicited reconsideration and a challenging of one's own deeply held convictions is about as radical as one can get before dressing up like a character from Mad Max and brawling in the streets.

THE PERILS OF ABSOLUTISM

Central to any ideology, is a sense of certainty. The notion that honest answers, wrought from a foundational bedrock of philosophical and political principles which are unto themselves providing of most any answer one could look for. For a prime example of this, consider American health care.

America is the greatest country on Earth...unless you're poor and sick.

Sure, technically speaking anyone, insured or not, rich or poor, can shuffle into any emergency room and receive care, but so often the peripheral realities to this go woefully unaddressed. From the individual or family bankruptcy that can result from an uninsured medical emergency, up through the driving up of overall costs as a result of either charitable care or simply unpaid medical debts, the simple financial and economic plights wrought from the for-profit model are as obscene as they are detrimental. And unlike many in the debates, some of whom see single payer as a step towards the dreaded red menace and others who equate the need for health care to shopping for furniture, I have personally lived through a rather damming experience myself with this industry and it's broader reaches.

In 2004, after kicking about in kitchens and call centers, I decided I wanted to further my education and enroll in college. By no means wealthy and coming from a family that was itself poverty stricken for many years, I like most students took out student loans in order to pay for tuition and materials. During my time in college I flourished, devouring the texts and maintaining a GPA somewhere in the vicinity of 3.7. I was invited to the Phi Beta Kappa honors society and penned countless essays, many of which served as templates for pieces to be later published in a number of smaller political journals.

Around this same time, I was stricken with an inexplicable and crippling chest pain which I couldn't explain or endure. Being without insurance as it was not provided by my employer at the time and too expensive for me to afford privately, I eventually wound up in the emergency room once my abilities to move and even breathe were hindered. Loaded up with pain killers, the doctors described the condition as unexplained chest wall inflammation and after a short round of medications, the pain subsided.

The problem arose after the repeated attempts to file the necessary paperwork for charitable care through the hospital proved fruitless. This effort, which required multiple attempts, as somehow the paperwork itself never seemed to make it to where it needed to be was quickly buried beneath what I can only describe as a mountain of bureaucratic inefficacy. It then was repeatedly lost in the process, causing my bill to eventually be shunted off into standard billing and upon my inability to pay taking its toll, collections. Repeated subsequent visits to the ER for the lancing of cysts and a recurring hematoma resulted in much the same.

Despite this, I was at the outset of my education. Having been assured that medical debt would not affect my ability to finance a degree program I found out in short order that by virtue of a Bush Administration effort to reform bankruptcy and student loan law, such was simply not the case.. After completing a year and a half at this small, commercial, community level school, I sought a more expansive substantive education and enrolled at Saint Anselm in a pre-law political science program.

After being almost immediately accepted into the rather prestigious school I worked closely with the financial aid office to secure the necessary funding through new loans and grant programs. Told initially that unless my parents were alumni, faculty or donors, or unless I played basketball, that there was no help to be found through the school itself, loans were again the only option. And after some shucking and jiving on the part of the financial aid department, I was told that the loans I needed were secured and I could begin classes when the new semester began. Unfortunately however, after that first semester, I was summoned to the registrars office and informed that unless I could produce $14,000, that my ability to continue beyond such was impossible.

Why? As it turned out, recent legislation at the time had made it easier for creditors to take medical debt into account, even when in respect to student aid. I, having never had a credit card, mortgage or bank loan of any kind outside of that in pursuit of education, was denied the ability to complete my degree because my outstanding medical debt made me ineligible for the necessary financing, even with a cosigner. Unceremoniously ejected from school for the twin curses of being poor and dogged by medical debt, I was left without a degree, without much in the way of a future and of course, over thirty thousand dollars in unpayable student debt.

And my story, you may be surprised to find, is far from isolated. Throughout the country medical debt dogs roughly 43 million Americans, with 2 million bankruptcies having resulted from such. One would think that with so many Americans finding their healthcare causing them greater financial and by extension, personal grief and problems than even housing, the nation would at some point get serious about tackling this issue.

There was a time, not all that long ago, when before strident talk of the intrinsic value of nationalism took hold, a more poignant and optimistic point of pride used to inhabit the patriotic American heart. This pride came from what is commonly referred to as the American spirit. A can-do attitude which said that no challenge was too great and no goal was out of reach for the plucky and industrious people of the United States. It was the attitude which both turned the nation into an economic and military superpower as well as placing human beings on the moon.

The notion was simple. Through grit, wit and a can-do attitude, not only could America do anything it set its collective mind to, but could do it better than any other nation on Earth. Curiously, or perhaps less than curious altogether, this classic can-do attitude does not seem to be as readily available these days, as overall faith in our institutions and cultural cohesion continues degrading. Still holding firm to the notion that America is a land of opportunity, a notable pessimism seems to have taken a rather selective hold in respect to what many Americans tend to think America is or is not capable of.

When asked about the topic of health care typically opinions are split. While a growing number of Americans, 56% according to a recent Kaiser Family Foundation poll, support the creation of a public Medicare For All single payer system, attitudes from those who oppose such remain as staunch as ever.

Often pointing to places such as the UK or Canada and speaking of endless wait times and unfathomable bureaucracy, this curious attitude towards single payer is one which almost comes across as defeatist at it's start. Leaving aside for the moment the moronic Randian arguments that all public services are forms of theft and that our system is ideal because it is private and for-profit, this curious notion that because, anecdotally, Britain and Canada have purportedly failed at providing such services – this being despite that the US is ranked 37th by the world health organization in respect to its system's effectiveness and doesn't even rank in the top 25 healthiest countries — that it would therefore be impossible for the US to effectively implement a public health care system.

So where in here is that famed American spirit? If we're to give the argument credit and not presume that such is rooted in a more ideological position on public services, business and government, is it not then curious to note that those who live and breathe the concept of American exceptionalism are utterly convinced that a thing can't work because in their eyes and according to their understanding, other countries couldn't make it work.

To be sure, in applying this notion that we as Americans cannot only do anything we set our minds to, but can do it better than anyone else, does it not stand to reason that wherever the roots of the purported failings of these others systems lie, that we ought be able to address such failings and create the ideal version of a system that others have failed to achieve?

The sad truth to this matter however, in the cases when such defenses of the current system are not rooted in the presumption that public health care systems are destined to fail on their own, is in my estimation far more ideological to a point of being outright profane.

Working on the Randian notion that any form of compulsory collectivism within a society is a gross violation of individual rights and the vaunted concept that greed, selfishness and selective indifference to the plights of others is itself a form of virtue. Many who oppose the notion of public health care systems do so for less than humanitarian reasons. Not rooted in a genuinely practical or pragmatic approach to the matter of health care itself, but rather from a position rooted more in blind sentimentality, the standard libertarian line in this case is simply that anything compulsory within society is by definition bad. Much like a stubborn adolescent who'll refuse to do what their told in school on the grounds that they don't like being told what to do, the notion of participation is null and void in their eyes, unless said participation in a system or institution is wholly voluntary and entirely private. Anything less is a form of oppression that they simply cannot tolerate.

Deflecting to notions of bake sale style charities for those in substantial need, the matter is less about the function of such a program and more about its form. The very idea of contributing to something for which they personally have no immediate need yet that will go to serve others who perhaps in their estimation don't work as hard, struggle as thoroughly or achieve by effort and merit to the same degree as they fancy themselves to have done, is such that stings with intolerable insult to the individualist absolutist. This being oddly just as effective a rebuke of the health insurance industry as it stands, the notion of every man being an island unto himself, accountable only to himself and responsible only for himself is one which while filling the mind with a righteous sense of rugged individualism, is sorely out of touch with the broader reality within which the individual resides.

To consider the nature of health insurance, we must first accept and admit that though private and for profit, two elements to the conventionally conservative mind which stand out as intrinsic virtues on their own, it is itself inherently collectivist. With the company acting as a broker, large numbers of individuals contribute to the financial resource pool that is meant to serve as a contingency for each member participating. For every hundred people paying in, when one falls ill or injured, the collective resources are used to pay for treatment, while the remaining balance paid in by the others ensures they will have access to such should the need arise.

Celebrated as this private collective formula is, with its underlying nature relying ostensibly on the proposed and to some, unassailable virtue of competition, it is fundamentally undercut by its most basic theory in this very same manner. In what way is a system that relies on the collective participation of the many for the contingent benefit of the few actually or functionally any different when made public? In what way is this system aided when substantial portions, or even marginal portions of the collective resources are allocated for the explicit purpose of enriching private individuals whose interests lie not with the provision of services, but the generation of profit and revenue, often at the expense of the service itself?

In what way is the theory of a broad and collective pool of resources being maintained aided when said pools are broken up into numerous smaller pools and manipulated by way of company policies to restrict and minimize the provision of services, not on any specific medical basis, but on the grounds that such helps maximize profitability and protect corporate assets? It has been reported that in 2017, the nation's top six health insurance companies reported six billion dollars in profits and across the board, CEO pay throughout the industry totaled $342.6 Million in the same year.

In what way, aside from espousing the spurious notions of corporate profits meaning a robust and healthy economy, can it be adequately argued that given the fundamental form and function of health insurance being that of a collective and contingent resource pool, that the deriving of such unfathomable private wealth from said pool in any way aids or benefits the provision of services that the industry itself is ostensibly meant to provide?

Furthermore, to cut to the heart of the arguments regarding health care spending and its essential place in our economy, one could easily say that if the building and maintaining of such a system is any form of lynch pin in respect to economic health, I would argue that it is in fact holding the economy hostage, rather than genuinely contributing to it. In much the same way that it is argued that anyone can get care and must merely run the risk of debt as a result should they be uninsured, the striking nature of how such ultimately inflates costs overall simply cannot be ignored.

Through and through, the arguments against a national health care program fall typically into the camps of a Randian antipathy towards government, a Calvanist attitude towards need and provision and a market oriented perspective in regards to what is a fundamental human need. All the while, the fact that individuals across the nation pay an average of $440 a month for individual coverage and upwards of $1200 for a family into these disparate and separated pools for services which not only incur endless amounts of ancillary costs, but have traditionally been held to ridiculous levels of internal corporate scrutiny so as to avoid having to pay for them at all should leave an honest and objective mind wondering exactly where the supposed benefit from this market oriented for profit system is derived.

Ultimately, this question which has in all honesty only scratched the surface of this issue, likewise serves as emblematic of its broader overall context. I can say I find no sense in the system which we have, nor derive any genuine respect for the piddling defenses of it. With the basic concept and theory to health insurance being what it is, the establishment of a larger, singular resource pool to ensure that those who need treatment can access it makes greater sense than handfuls of smaller pools designed ostensibly to do the same thing.

The dedication of these funds being set exclusively to the administration and provision of services without the demands for private profit makes greater sense than ensuring that substantial amounts of said funds go to line the pockets of people who have nothing to do with the provision of said services. The assurance of access to medical treatment without the mountains of personal debt that can come along with such if one is uninsured makes greater sense than making medical treatment itself something one is forced to weigh as they might the purchase of a car.

And beyond moral or ethical judgments about whether medicine and medical treatment ought to be seen as a public service or not, the provision of such to the population can ensure that this, the supposedly greatest nation on Earth, can not only ensure better overall public health, but can prove instrumental in ensuring that disease and sickness do not have the chances to spread as widely as they do without such. Some may argue that public health services would make slaves of medical providers, obligating them to render services that ought to be viewed as the province of their own labors against their will. Aside from the fetid hyperbole of such a suggestion though, within both the choice to become physicians or surgeons, as well as within the very oath of Hippocrates they swear to, the ambition of such practices is not one of business, but is itself the business of healing.

"Into whatsoever houses I enter, I will enter to help the sick, and I will abstain from all intentional wrong-doing and harm, especially from abusing the bodies of man or woman, bond or free. And whatsoever I shall see or hear in the course of my profession, as well as outside my profession in my intercourse with men, if it be what should not be published abroad, I will never divulge, holding such things to be holy secrets."

In this fourth passage of the Hippocratic oath, we can see plain as day "Into whatsoever houses I enter, I will enter to help the sick, and I will abstain from all intentional wrong-doing and harm, especially from abusing the bodies of man or woman, bond or free." Nowhere in this oath are words related to payments, debts, profits or riches owed mentioned and nowhere in this oath is the sickly and perverse Randian notion of universal commodification referenced in the slightest.

Even within the updated text, the words read *"I will prevent disease whenever I can, for prevention is preferable to cure. I will remember that I remain a member of society, with special obligations to all my fellow human beings, those sound of mind and body as well as the infirm.*

If I do not violate this oath, may I enjoy life and art, respected while I live and remembered with affection thereafter. May I always act so as to preserve the finest traditions of my calling and may I long experience the joy of healing those who seek my help."

If you can find anywhere in these words, dear listener, anything referencing or suggesting that the treating of the ill or infirmed is more business than service, I encourage you to point such out. However as I am confident you will find none, let us set aside these backwards claims and remember fundamentally that the act of putting a price on the health and wellbeing of our fellow human beings is among the most craven and despicable acts one can engage in.

THE ABSOLUTES OF PERIL

As with most things of a dynamic or conceptual nature, these truths tend to go both ways. For example, the simple selection of another altogether basic hot button issue offers up a similar albeit different ideological blindness when it comes to its debate. This example with which one can drive this point home, which likewise often proves to be as divisive if not more so than the healthcare system that is so often tasked with addressing its routine outcomes, is guns.

It would take a rather extreme naiveté for anyone paying attention to deny that the United States has a rather serious gun violence problem. Ranking 31st in the world for deaths due to gun violence, with this ranking counting war torn areas as well as nations with extreme levels of poverty and crime, the most advanced and prosperous superpower in human history is also seen by many as being one of the most violent. While a dire issue to be sure, the left versus right mentality so many adopt unquestioningly seems to perpetually lead discussions of such matters down some of the stalest and most predictable paths imaginable, with many who jump into this 'arena' boiling down the question of a solution to either more or less guns.

Why though, as the left demands guns be either heavily regulated or banned outright and the right insists we simply need more guns to shoot the bad guys dead and serve as a 'deterrent,' is one entire half of the matter itself seemingly ignored outright? I'm speaking of course of the 'violence' portion to the 'gun violence' epidemic. In the same spirit that London just last year surpassed New York City in regards to its own violence problem without guns being a central factor, so too do countless other countries with widespread gun ownership see little in the way of violence comparatively themselves.

While both sides in this unending and often very bitter battle over policy do often like to trot out these matters in various capacities, always hoping and insisting that they support their own perspectives, a glazed and sometimes dumbfounded look crosses their faces when asked to consider the facts on hand without the guns themselves being a factor. When asked to consider the underlying question of violence itself, the words "I hadn't really thought of that" are often sometimes the best you can hope for, with this consideration itself not even being central to the point at hand. The point here is more in fact that within the generally intractable positions people seems happy to put themselves in, in regards to their thinking, merely suggesting a different perspective beyond the polarized two on offer very often seems to strike the true believer as either an unnecessary and irrelevant suggestion, or one which strikes them as though it were a grand epiphany.

In 2016 studies found that six nations produced a solid half of the world's gun related deaths, with the United States ranking just below Brazil and just above Mexico, Venezuela, Colombia and Guatemala. Not exactly the sorts of countries one would expect the world's greatest and most prosperous super-power to be classed with.

However for decades now, pushing properly into generations worth of debate and discussion, the extraordinary levels of gun violence in the US have spurned many into calls for tough action to regulate, control or even ban firearms for civilian use. With gun control advocates pointing to places such as the U.K. and Australia as examples of how their bans drastically and almost entirely reduced or eliminated gun crime, calls for such to take place in the U.S. have become rallying cries for the progressive left. With the rise of the celebrity survivor such as David Hogg and Emma Gonzales, who in our voracious media climate were thrust into the public eye following the mass shooting at Stoneman Douglas High School in 2018, much of the modern attention in respect to gun crime tends to be less upon the average everyday violence in places like Chicago, Baltimore or New Orleans and now more focused upon the seemingly and increasingly regular stories of mass shootings.

Regardless though, the debate itself is possibly among the most contentious of our modern age, with hardliners on the left calling for bans and regulation citing the mass killings, often of young people in the course of their studies, and hardliners on the right often calling for more guns so as to turn ordinary people into guardian "good guys." While those in favor of gun control cite foreign nations bans, those opposed cite the second amendment. Yet in the zeal and enthusiasm with which each side trots out these lines, so much is lost in the process.

Firstly, in respect to the often cited if not fetishized second amendment to the US Constitution, an important and honestly glaring oversight on the part of gun rights advocates comes by way of their obsessive invocation and generally erroneous reading of such. Though in the course of judicial interpretation the phrase "shall not be infringed" has been itself adjudicated to declare that firearms ownership is itself a right of the public, the historical context of the amendment is often conveniently overlooked. With the nation having been founded originally upon the concepts of popular sovereignty according to (small-r) republican theory, the original intent behind the "well regulated militia" clause (*the very clause often overlooked, ignored or misinterpreted by gun enthusiasts*) spoke less to the rugged individualist notion that the protection of one's self and family relied on their access to weapons and more on original intent in regards to national defense. An often forgotten precept to republican theory states that the maintaining of a standing military is itself often a greater threat to liberty and popular sovereignty than are potential foreign invaders. This being due largely to man's long history of having governments and republics overtaken by the orderly and powerful military institutions created either for defense or conquest in the past.

It can be and is often is exceptionally easy for Americans, with our civilian controlled military apparatus, to forget that throughout much of history and much of the world today, military power is often something separate from civilian governments and that often when one hears of a military coup, usually in places such as Africa, Asia or South America, it is often military leaders assuming power from either weak or corrupt civilian governments, or from the hands of previous military dictators.

Likewise, with a parallel history of strong central governments, such as those of monarchs often using soldiers as a means to maintain power over their civilian populations, the existence of a standing army was doubly seen as a serious threat to the sustained liberty and popular sovereignty of a free people. As such, at the time of the founding, general ambitions were to disband the army after the revolution had come to a close, very akin to historical English theory which stated that armies should be raised only in times when they were obviously needed, with the maintaining of state and municipal civil militias to remain on the ready for the expressed purposes of providing for the ordinary common defense.

In such times when conscription for service was common to the point of being nearly universal, participation in militia activities was seen as a matter of civic duty and was, with few exceptions for the mad, the disabled and the infirmed, expected for men and boys of fighting age and fitness. Seen then not only as means by which to provide for common defense, military or militia service was also seen a manner to instill discipline, bearing and good conduct throughout life, which themselves were each seen as central civic virtues.

Much in opposition to common thought of our modern age, private firearms ownership, while not uncommon, was far from widespread, usually by simple virtue of their cost and, absent any genuine domestic manufacturing base for guns, their effective scarcity. With the majority of such being imports at the time, it would not be until the American Civil War that the large scale manufacturing of American guns would even really begin.

Often, for municipal militia provision, a stock of muskets would be often kept and maintained by a militia quartermaster, held in the common trust and ownership of the civilian authorities, but not specifically belonging to any individual or family. Through drill and ceremony, the assigning of and respect for rank and position and the readiness to lay down one's life in service to their fellows, these senses of duty and service were as central to the concept of patriotism as they are today, albeit on a different scale, rooted usually in somewhat different moti-

Laughter of a Scoundrel | 29

vations. As such, the presumption on the part of many founding era patriots was that once the war with England had come to its conclusion, military service would again revert to the organization and maintenance of the militia.

It was only due to the largely untold realities faced by the fledgling United States following the close of its war for independence that the continued funding and organization of a national military apparatus remained. This being the result of rather revisionist versions of our national history, often tending to frame the war and America's victory as decisive and glorious, the muddied and complicated realities found in historical accounts written at the time of its happening paint a much different picture. In addition Washington's own army, which is generally portrayed as steely eyed and determined to the last man, actually being one which was rife with malprovision, disease, lacking in funding, suffering desertion rates upwards of a full third of its original force and suffering from much of the same sorts of congressional bickering over supply and provision as we've seen in more modern wars, the continued presence of a massive British military force just to the north in Canada made the immediate dissolving of what standing military forces the U.S. had after Cornwallis' surrender in 1781 a less appealing notion than most republicans cared for.

With the Constitution's ratification in 1788 and the Bill of Rights ratification in 1791 (based originally on George Masons Virginia Declaration of Right from 1776,) with the continued hopes of returning to a civilian militia based system of defense, the second amendment was included to address one central objection made by the Anti-Federalist movement to ensure defense remained in control of the states and not the federal government. As rooted in original fears of central authority taking too strong a hand, many modern gun rights supporters insist that the central purpose to the second amendment was to allow for a civilian overthrow of the federal government should it take its presumptions of authority too far. A claim that is effectively castrated upon the simple consideration of what good an AR-15 would do against a guided missile or Apache helicopter attack, regardless of whether it possesses a forward grip and thirty round magazine.

Beyond these often historically inaccurate arguments however, perhaps the saddest opposition to gun control which is not rooted in historical interpretation of founding era mythology, comes more from an internal struggle within pro-gun communities over acknowledgement of rather basic control measures, many of which are already in practice throughout many parts of the country. When the questions arise surrounding the matters of background checks, waiting periods and licensing, many of the most hard core gun rights advocates tend to regard anything of the sort as intrinsically infringing on their rights to bear arms.

Rooted in a more strident libertarianism, there are many who propose in accordance with notions of civilian heroes gunning down "bad guys" when things go awry that mandating things such as registration, screening protocols, safety instruction or licensing, much as we presently do in relation to the rights of citizens to drive on public roads, that such are merely steps taken by an intrinsically authoritarian big-brother government to prepare for confiscations and subjugation of the population at large. Ignoring that in a 2015 survey of gun owners carried out by "Public Policy Polling," that eighty-three percent of respondents favored universal background checks for gun purchases and that of them, twenty four percent identified as members of the National Rifle Association, with roughly seventy-two percent of that group responding the same. This perception is not as widely shared in common debate. In this, the most hardcore gun rights enthusiasts – those being who we as usual, find presented as emblematic of the broader demographic— often insist that any attempt by the government to control the sale and flow of guns is inherently unconstitutional. These same figures presented themselves previously in a 2012 poll carried out by Republican pollster Frank Luntz working with an even larger sample size.

All the same however, as judicial interpretation over the years has made civilian firearms ownership a declared right of the populace on its own, a sincere lack of genuine judicial awareness (or at least argument and expression thereof) on the part of many hardcore second amendment enthusiasts is often overshadowed by the more general ideological and philosophical adherences to such being a right than the fundamental understanding of how and why such is so in the first place. In this selective misrepresentation of founding intent and philosophy, a genuine opportunity to leverage better arguments in regards to matters ranging from simple practicality to the underlying matter of whether the "gun violence" problem in the U.S. has more to do with violence itself than the tools with which it's carried out tend to remain inert within the broader dialogue. Likewise this cutting off at the knees of deeper conversations in the modern public square is far from limited to those in favor of gun rights and in fact infects their opposition almost as much, if not more so, within the ranks of their opposition.

To take up the more common anti-gun arguments, we should first look to the notion of foreign actions taken. In respect to foreign gun bans or controls, though shooting deaths in the U.K. have dropped to an average of one in one million, knife crime and deaths due to bladed weapons have skyrocketed to a point that 2018 London witnessed homicide rates surpass those of New York City.

In Australia, though guns are not entirely banned outright, the tight restrictions and licensing requirements has likewise fueled a downward overall trend in gun violence, while bladed homicides remain overall consistent with a few spikes and valleys observable over a fifteen year period of observation. When looking over such statistics, though tight gun controls can in those cases result in a drop in gun violence itself, overall violence rates tend to follow trends of their own with a most notable aspect to them being rises in violent crime during periods of observable economic or political stresses.

Though through media we are often lead to believe that mass shootings are an epidemic in relation to gun crime, studies of data wrought from the FBI Uniform Crime Reporting Program find that such incidents only account for two percent of all gun deaths. When broader data is considered, we find that cities with populations of 250,000 or higher experience murder rates in general that are generally several orders of magnitude above national averages. Likewise while the much decried AR-15 "assault rifle" is generally held up as a mass murder weapon requiring immediate banning, the vast majority of shootings in the U.S. are carried out with ordinary shotguns and handguns.

Often stating in their own invocations of the second amendment that the founders, with their muskets and flintlock pistols likely "didn't have assault weapons in mind" when they enshrined the civilian right to arms into the Constitution, the fundamental concept of permitting the civilian population to remain armed goes itself unaddressed as pitiful interpretations are offered suggesting that such was intended for hunting or frontier purposes. Missing the mark as to the central nature of military application as intended in its day, these strident activists likewise serve in their advocacy to muddy the waters of historical understanding, generally serving to deepen the divide with every passing utterance.

Yet, just as their opposition in their vocal minorities often fail to realize that perhaps managing gun sales and ownership in a manner similar to that of driving privileges could ultimately prove to be a boon to the social legitimacy of gun ownership, the orthodoxy rejects this outright. Though perhaps appearing to be sensible to many, these potential steps that could be taken are likewise ignored by the more vocal campaigners. This being that with many anti-gun advocates, with their own narratives often dominated by the most aggressive and fashionably outraged voices, their arguments routinely fail to adequately address the simple reality that in a nation with three hundred and ninety three million guns, many owned by those who profess that they'll only be taken "over their dead bodies," that confiscations, bans and rounds up are as unfeasible and impossible as are the fantasies that a universally armed public would somehow stem the issues of gun violence.

With both of these sides lined up, often online before such spills into the streets in usually garish and unproductive mass demonstrations ranging from protest walks to open carry dick-waving, getting to the heart of the matter can seem almost impossible. With so little said about how economic and socio-economic realities play into the proliferation of violence as a whole, how the manufactured American ethos of frontier mentalities insisting both that threats await around every corner and that only through being armed can one protect themselves and the self-fulfilling prophecies of presumed escalations of force, violence and overall hostility, is can be of little wonder why such little progress has been made in respect to these matters. This of course is not to say however that none is in fact being made.

Contrary to popular belief, overall rates of violence and victimization throughout the United States and especially in urban areas where such tends to be several orders of magnitude worse, have been on a generally steady decline since the early 1990s. Though murder rates in hotspots such as Chicago and Baltimore remain highly publicized, statistical data shows steady and noted overall decreases in such spanning several years. While tougher law enforcement practices in general could be said to be the cause of such, neither strict gun regulation nor a proliferation of guns can either be credited with these declines.

As becomes evident with nearly any other hot-button issue under debate, the realities and nuances are often lost beneath the din of absolutist orthodoxies which insist, usually upon ideological grounds, that there is only one correct way to move forward and that nothing else will suffice. For every argument offered one way, an equally if not more bombastic claim is usually waiting to be lobbed back over the wall in a continuous and unending set of volleys. Often aimed more at destroying the opposition than really striking to any fundamental truths, it makes greater sense as to why such arguments tend to go nowhere. Likewise with high profile stories of police shootings of often unarmed black youths, claims by many self-appointed racial justice advocates that the United States is a "white supremacist" nation remain dubious as regular nationwide criminal justice reforms work to remediate the lingering strands of historical state oppression and a growing middle and upper class within those communities continues to rise.

Now not to be mistaken, none of this is to say there aren't serious and pressing issues facing our nation. Much to the contrary racial divisions and unequal treatment both legally and economically do still exist and lead to countless ruined lives, broken homes and denials of brighter futures. However much in the same way that many crusaders operating with absolutist mindsets of this way or that leap at the chance to parade a headline around as evidence as to just how correct they are, the volume with which such crusaders and absolutists insist on being heard makes the sorts of quiet, respectful and factually oriented conversations required to get to the real bottoms of these matters all the more difficult.

Fueled by a high octane mix of ideology and absolute certainty and propagated endlessly by a sensationalist media and an equally hysterical social media, the roads to solutions to the serious and dire problems we face are quite often mined with the explosive rhetoric of absolutists and opportunists who see these hills to climb more as stages from which to preach their often fallacious or misguided rhetorical "truths."

Though an average and reasonable person, even when faced with someone who is diametrically opposed to their positions, can sit and have something of a productive discussion, those who follow absolutists or champion absolutism itself will continually get in the way. Until we are able as a nation and a society to knock such charlatans, provocateurs, ideologues and absolutists out of our way, personal certainty will continually be mistaken for insight, stridency for conviction and perhaps worst of all, ideological absolutism for sound and reasoned philosophy, these endless cycles of shrill screaming matches will almost certainly keep real debate on the fringes.

THE CULTURE WAR RUINS EVERYTHING

So you may have likely seen or heard reference to this matter for quite a long time now. To my own recollection, the first time a "culture war" was referenced by a public personality or pundit was likely Bill O'Reilly and his book "Culture Warrior," where he extols the virtues of his strident conservatism while attempting to lay the blame for every conceivable evil at the feet of those damned liberals. To be sure, at the time the landscape was, while similar, also quite different.

In those days it was typically the conservative right who demanded strict laws and restrictions to enforce preferred cultural norms, stirring up moral panics and relying on emotionally laden rhetoric to advance their preferred message. Contrasted against this was a liberal intelligentsia who seemed to enjoy touting a smug intellectualism as their default mode of operation, rolling their eyes at the "bible thumpers" and "retrograde knuckle-draggers" and their senses of tradition or faith. However to those not old enough to remember such times, it might almost seem unlikely or impossible for what is effectively a fundamental shift to have flipped matters so thoroughly upside down.

Whereas in the honestly recent past, a moral panic from a blustering lunatic like Glen Beck was contrasted against the snide dismissiveness of someone like Bill Maher, we now find the grating "wokeness" and insane ramblings of Salon columnists battling against the sneering smugness of Ben Shapiro. While in the past the liberal left, usually touting higher levels of formal education and often speaking from positions of what would later be called "privilege" would derisively relish conservative lamentation of a changing cultural or political landscape, we now have "liberal tears" being a sadly apt meme throughout the right and even in more moderate circles who see the new neo-progressive leftist ideology as obscene and reactionary. Even here though, we can see as recently as 2011 fissures within the political left which seemed to precipitate this shift, with the once dry and condescending writers such as Chris Hedges lording an apparent sense of progressive sophistication even over other liberals with less strident identity focuses such as Sam Harris.

Within all of these shifts in approach and demeanor and decorum occurring between the proverbial left and right, even within their own contained factions, we see the growth of what now generally (and in some cases intentionally) refer to as "the culture war." Regarding the left and right in proverbial senses here for the reason of their tactics, focus and overall personalities shifting like rudderless sailboats upon the open ocean, these terms themselves often do little to truly define an actual thought or thought process as much as to define a side one aligns with in varying degrees in their self-sustaining warfare for the soul and control of culture. Yet from this, a series of self-fulfilling prophecies seem to emerge with regularity, leading us down a road where the only guiding light is an insistence that it's darker elsewhere.

But the roots of this inanity set aside for the moment, the net effects ought to, at least according to a rational mind, outweigh whatever supposed gains or victories or even virtues the warriors clashing over the culture claim to be fighting for. Whether it is the damage this endless and increasingly obnoxious culture war has inflicted on our entertainment and art, such as films, music, literature and the like, or alternately the fundamental divisions such has sewn even within families, the only gains actually made in any real capacity for either side seem to come in the form of personal elevation and exaltation of those leading the charges. Be they the wokest blogger calling for diversity in science fiction, or the snarkiest YouTube critic insisting that post-modern communist plots rest behind every leftist utterance, it is the personal profiles of those engaged in the "fight" which seem to be the most elevated at the end of the day, with the ideas typically being reduced to bare essence, dried out, packaged in bright colors and sold off like political bouillon cubes.

Meanwhile, as some seek to raise armies and hell over the use of gendered pronouns and others still seem to base the entirety of their political thought on how poorly it'd be received by those on the "other side," the lengths and reach of fringe and radical factions seems to grow daily. Whereas in the past a radical leftist was often seen as an eco-warrior who'd perhaps read half of Das Kapital before dawning a Che t-shirt, they now pale in comparison to the violent and erratic chapters of Antifa with their "black bloc" tactics and gleeful engagement in violence. Likewise on the right, whereas religious fundamentalists or anti-government separatists were seen as the defined fringe, we now see ultra nationalist and ethno-nationalist groups forming and growing, often under the banner of combatting the growing scourge of presumed communist leftism.

These groups and fringes feed not only off of one another, claiming their actions as a response to those of their counterparts, but also and primarily through the pitched fervor of our evolving "culture war." In the same respect here that "centrism" is viewed and used as a dirty or derogatory term by many who are not necessarily even on the fringes themselves, the existence of such radicals, spurned by over-stated cultural panics has increasingly fed a common notion that in this war one must pick a side as a lesser of two evils, with no real wiggle room to be found. Though seldom stated outright, the spokespeople and figureheads who lead or inspire these factions generally help to establish such a bicameral notion of perpetual banality through their consistent representation of the worst elements on the other side as being emblematic of that side as a whole.

The culture war, in which we are all seemingly expected to participate, is an entirely self-perpetuating nightmare of division and reductionist thinking. Beyond merely growing the scope and size of radical fringes, by virtue of its simplified presentation of what is otherwise complicated and dynamic thought, the war they wage makes the very act of discussing politics with friends, family or strangers an invitation to abject disaster. It is within the clashing of hysterical moral panics, smug dehumanizing derision and prideful insistence on not giving the opposing side so much as the benefit of a doubt, that the concept of ideological contention blowing up into outright ideological warfare is not an unrealistic notion.

But how else does this insipid contest of vapid sloganeering ruin the world we inhabit? Surely as life extends beyond political discussions and works of fiction, there must be some elements of 'everything' that aren't ruined.

Certainly the matter of family or kinship with close friends exists above and beyond the reach of such inanity.

In general, yes. True bonds between people do tend to survive the petty nonsense that is the politics of division. However just as with social media, the nature of the red versus blue, left versus right, woke versus based nonsense is such that to the true believer, not even familial connection can necessarily survive. Consider the simpering nonsense on offer from people like Stefan Molyneaux, who openly calls for people to abandon friends and family for holding different opinions. Compare this to the hysteria that seems to embody the anti-Trump "resistance" and the slew of articles from ideological propaganda sources such as Salon, The Mary Sue and so on, stating that one should not date, speak to, befriend or remain close with those who support the Trump regime.

Through and through the two sides to these insipid conflicts and the myriad of factions which comprise them seem beyond eager to not only mirror and replicate the actions and rhetoric of their opposition, but to take them even further whenever possible. These warring tribes of true believers not only enjoy such for the ostensible effectiveness they presume of them, but take absolutely no qualms in sinking even lower, pointing across the no-man's land towards the trenches of their enemies and loudly proclaiming that "they did it first." Participants here are then seemingly compelled to run in a race to the bottom, fueled by the petty justifications of feuding five year olds in a school yard, with gripes and points of ire so banal the grocery store tabloids of old would probably find them too petty to print.

Beyond the specious arguments, the irrelevant sources of scorn, the corruption and poisoning of nearly every fandom, environment, subculture or movement the competing sides can get their pudgy hands clasped around, a deeper and more insidious cycle and affect are propelled by this ever expanding ideological slap fight. These are the distractions of an 'end-of-the-empire' type of common mentality. Often regarded as "bread and circuses," the endless and typically futile arguments over representation in media from the left, or the often nebulous 'preserving our culture' notions espoused by elements on the right, often by simply virtue of volume and din, seem to dominate much of the public discourse in certain circles.

This is not to say that such facile nonsense is all encompassing, but rather it stands as emblematic of the nature of the struggle. From both sides, the deeper and more meaningful and menacing issues faced by the world go often unaddressed by these politically attuned movements. For the left, while classic matters of corporate influence over elections and legislation take a back seat to moral panics over identity politics centered on victimhood culture, the same mechanisms and catalysts for the wars, corporate handouts, tax breaks and so on which traditionally moved the liberal or progressive scene not only continue along their ways, but grow in scope and power as a result. Likewise for the right, whereas free speech and expression ought to rest at the heart of any civil libertarian movement, a great deal of such is focused more on providing shielding from the more guttural, hateful and juvenile imbecility than articulating the true value and nature of free expression itself.

The adage that the most reprehensible speech requires and deserves the most strident protection is true. When any expression is banned or suppressed, a precedent is set that will almost inevitably be expanded on if left undefeated. Much in the same way that efforts to discuss real matters of police, housing or economic reform for impoverished areas are ignored in favor of the more fashionable outrage spurned by movements such as those which have risen from seemingly nowhere in just this last decade, so too are fights in favor of free speech undermined when the focus becomes exalting and defending the unlettered stooges who spout of edgy or racist garbage with the same glee that a primary school hooligan might repeatedly blurt out the word "penis" for a pointless chuckle.

All the while however, basic and fundamental rights continue to be stripped down and eroded, ironically enough by both left and right depending on who is in power and how said acts support and advance their narratives. Gone are the days when the mainstay of progressive or liberal concern focused on the still standing violations of our privacy lost in the wake of 9/11. Replacing them we instead have routine calls for censorship and speech codes, all with the aims of potentially protecting delicate emotions, none of which are likely to matter in an Orwellian surveillance state. Whereas conservative values have for the better part of a century dictated that government intervention in the affairs of private businesses was to be avoided at all cost, the enthusiastic zeitgeists of modern conservatism as shaped by the Trump phenomenon has even lead some so-called conservatives to support the assaults on press and social media companies, with some even supporting Trump's suggestions to create a state run media.

Within the ever increasing pitch and fervor of what are often superficial, simple minded and singularly stupid political trends, it becomes hard not to compare such to some terrifying blend of professional sports and reality television. Gone now are the days when people such as Gore Vidal and William Buckley, in the midst of a genuine intellectual clash worth note and respect, shocked the audiences of their time, with what by comparison to modern standards was a tame and trifling moment of animosity. To say in the context of this comparison that decorum is what has been lost would itself fall short of the mark, as even in respect to the most basic levels of intellect and poise on offer, expectations have been largely lowered to a point in which intellectual clashes are viewed more like professional wrestling matches.

Consider the average report or headline should a debate or discussion take place in the public eye. With so little generally said in depth about the subject matter or context of arguments posed, people typically look to see how Ben Shapiro "destroyed" an opponent or how Rachel Maddow "owns" a commentator. Despite the "arguments" typically being little more than the recitation of stale talking points, even the fundamental purpose of public debates has changed. Just as we will not likely see a new Vidal or Buckley rising to the place of thought leader for the partisan scenes, we shall be just as unlikely to see another Christopher Hitchens rise in the realm of cultural critique.

Though it was certainly not he who said such first, many defer to his words in respect to the purpose of debate being to convince the undecided in earshot and not simply put down your opponent to the applause of a guffawing following. This seems to have become the nature of public disagreement in that the "owned/destroyed/eviscerated" clickbait headlines that announce such seem in many cases to have turned debates into competing rallies in which sycophants and true believers cluster together in the hopes of having their beliefs yet again reaffirmed to the sounds of hoots and applause.

These desires by the hardcore devotees of modern ideology extend beyond merely attending talks by their preferred media darlings in a way eerily similar to those of big tent revivals. The insistence that in this epic struggle that is the modern culture war, the routine maligning of any who fail to fall within the parameters of their established and preferred orthodoxies are often viewed as either potential converts or heretics, spitting in the face of the grand truth they've discovered. Comparisons in this respect to religious zealotry aren't difficult to make and are generally lamentably accurate. Replace god's will with the blind insistence of opinion being fact. Replace the saints and their deeds with often dead philosophers and the reductionist Cliff's Notes versions of their perspectives. Replace prayer with rhetoric, commandment with doctrine and the pulpit with a news desk and soon ideology becomes indistinguishable from religion.

ANTI-SOCIAL MEDIA

If you're to ask the average culture warrior what began and what continues to enflame these divisions, you're very likely to hear that it was "the other guys" who were responsible. Whether this claim asserts that it was racist Nazi Trump supporters opposing feminism and civil rights, or inversely the dastardly social justice warriors seeking to destroy free speech, the answers will inevitably rest with the given gladiator's nemesis and their subversive crusades. Yet beyond these generally petty attempts to frame each step of understanding of the problem, there exists a singular and binding constant between them. This constant is, as the title to this chapter suggest, social media.

Considering the nature of these new platforms of communication, which not only continue to evolve daily in respect to form and function but also serve as some of the primary battlegrounds for matters of hostility and division, we can see quite plainly that the double edged nature to this sword is something we are still only now coming to fully understand. With studies from universities and research institutes as well as common opinion polls routinely highlighting the often darker nature to social media use and engagement, those who use platforms such as Facebook, Twitter, Instagram or the like, are routinely finding their own observations validated when findings that regular use can lead to or enhance things such as depression and anxiety. Before even considering the political aspects and social media's role in stoking the fires of what are often very petty political divisions, the fundamental realities to these rapidly evolving platforms must be addressed.

So let us for the moment consider social media in the context of real world environments. While Facebook is largely a platform regarded by many as the sometimes only means by which people can stay in contact with friends and family, Twitter is something far more public in its nature. In order for a post or comment to come across your view in the former it is generally required that there be some connection between you and the person posting it. Whether this is due to its having been shared by a common contact or merely something seen as posted by someone you're already connected to, Facebook offers a slightly, albeit not entirely closed network in comparison to Twitter. Twitter inversely is something which allows anyone the potential and ability to reach millions upon millions of users reliant less on one's own connections and instead dependent on the numbers of shares a given post is afforded based simply on who sees it and when.

In this context we could view Twitter a public square in contrast to Facebook which is a bit more like a dinner table occupied by friends, family and acquaintances. Now due largely to their immediacy in respect to one's ability to compose a thought and express it to the world, neither of these networks offer or promote any obligation to really consider what is being said or shared, leaving such expressly in the hands of the user themselves. With the fast and rapidly increasing pace of the world we seem to be building, the very notion of thinking before you speak is something fewer and fewer people take the time to do. In a time of "hot takes" and "tl;dr" (too long, didn't read for those unaware) wherein guttural terseness is often preferred to more thoughtful long form expression, the act of thinking minimally and speaking briefly routinely reduces the value and depth of our communications, often resulting in either tragic misunderstandings or needless, intentional provocations.

Search in recent memory if you can think of a time either you or someone you know severed ties with a family member or close friend over a bitter difference of opinion on Facebook. Whether a blustering and reactive opinion or merely a harmless expression of perhaps an idle thought, comment wars have become so common that many seeking to avoid these conflagrations have made it a personal policy to avoid posting anything of meaning or perspective at all. With a simple miscalculated expression of thought on the matter of a news story or election, the apparent eagerness of many to willfully misrepresent ideas is often part and parcel with an attempt to appear bold and strident in one's convictions. This fundamentally simple act however, often serves as a catalyst to end otherwise meaningful relations.

At least, on Facebook in this respect. Likewise, with the recent spate of off color jokes or poorly devised tweets on the parts of actors, writers, directors, musicians, comedians and various other artists and public personalities serving to in some cases utterly destroy their careers, the courts of public opinion have found in social media the means to exact bitter consequences for what are often merely inane or innocuous utterances. Here, we find that just as these mediums can allow for thoughtless speech or expression trotted out into the world as genuine conviction, so too do we see that they open up the doors to vicious exploitation by parties seeking to signal to their world their virtues, or merely play a part in another's downfall, often merely as a means to exact and feel a sense of power. Between these two, taking the analogies of private dinner tables versus public squares, Facebook is often a vehicle by which one can befoul, offend and alienate their closer connections, while Twitter affords that same opportunity in the broader public.

Leaving now the established notion of division in this sense aside for the moment, we can also consider the overall cheapening of personal connections that has evolved as a byproduct of the rapid pace and thoughtless nature to these services. With the first generations coming of age with these platforms being standard methods of social interaction, many view the value of friendships to rest more in the quantity than the quality of such, with one's numbers of friends and followers coming to serve as markers of personal merit and value. With some accounts on Facebook maintaining thousands upon thousands of connections and having them labeled "friends," the innate desire within many for fame and notoriety becomes intrinsically linked to both the scope of one's profile as well as their sense of self worth.

With the estimated number of maximum relationships the human being can enjoy (this being known as Dunbar's number,) being approximately one hundred and fifty, the concept of one having thousands upon thousands of actual friends is laughable at best. With young people increasingly being raised online, these concepts of public profiles being connected to the values of human connections, stands as somewhat threatening to the common humanity which for some is often difficult if not impossible to truly understand. For many who perhaps make their connections using social media, a temporary and interchangeable nature to their bonds with others can often weaken whatever connections they make, causing said "friendships" to be disposable and reliant on timing and convenience as opposed to being deeply reaching and genuinely meaningful.

CYCLES OF COMMON THOUGHT

In their considerations, many who look at the evolving trends within political and ideological movements often defer to the notion of the swinging pendulum effect. In this it is asserted that for every swing to one side, a responding swing back to the other is to be expected. Should a decade or era experience a strong liberal or leftist insurgence within the common dialogue, the expectation of a resulting right wing or conservative rise is for the most part, assured. Likewise in the inverse, given time.

In this analysis there often remains a somewhat waning hope that as the 'pendulum' swings in this regard, that eventually as all objects in motion beneath the pull of gravity will do, will lose momentum and eventually come to rest in something of a center. Setting aside the acidic reaction to the very notion of centrism as described earlier, it is the general hope that following a bout of political fringes vying for domination of a dialogue that a more rational and reasonable movement, inspiring a more rational and reasonable tone will emerge, allowing society to enjoy a more stable environment of peace and prosperity. This notion, though rooted in what one might regard as a sensible perspective given the physical manifestation of the idea itself as a swinging pendulum in this sense, is as equally optimistic as it is utterly misguided.

Absent physical laws such as those of gravity and momentum, this metaphorical pendulum is one which rather than losing momentum upon each swing, tends instead to gain it, allowing the back swing from left or right to reach further in the opposite direction as it goes. This is itself due to the cyclical nature of political hostility and factional divides. As ideology itself generally relies upon people being too busy or too distracted to dwell deeply on the questions of their age and provides for them a ready-made set of answers and positions built more around a general idea or sentiment than empirical reason, its inherent failures are typically the most effective vehicles for advancing its opposing counterparts. Even, in many cases, if they themselves are equally horrid.

Just as political victories can inspire the rise of radical factions from left or right with the feeling within said circles that such is "their time," so too can defeats drive true believers even deeper into the mire that is their ideological framework. In some cases, political losses can even inspire a hardening of resolve as the losers in such instances are granted by virtue of their loss the sense of being rebel underdogs fighting against what they come to view as the tyrannical power wielded by their opposition. Naturally the depth of conviction regarding the merit of power itself lasts only as long as defeat is sustained, however in both victory and defeat the true believers and those who follow them are never short on means to validate and justify their beliefs, finding such to be just as readily on tap when power changes hands.

Should a left wing government come into power and fail to live up to the lofty ideals expressed by the leaders spearheading whatever movement it may be, the inevitable failures to live up to such grand and sweeping promises often leaves a bitter taste in the mouths of voters and political classes. When coupling these inevitable failures to deliver upon what was promised with the generally reactionary nature of the masses as a whole, the shifts in sentiment within those not so truly devout in their ideals is rather easily observed. From the supposed liberalism of Bill Clinton, the US then found fervor and enthusiasm for the neoconservative nationalism of the Bush administration. This fervor then dying down and withering, the nation then enthusiastically embraced the supposed progressivism of Barack Obama, followed then as we know with a disenchanted and divided nation soon finding a gaudy and generally obnoxious thrill in the blustering conservatism of Donald Trump.

Yet beyond even these electoral examples, looking to the rises of the regressive left and alt-right allows us an even more direct series of such instances with the most common refrain from the activist and pundit sets of these respective sides citing frustration and hostility towards the other as being a central motivation for their adoptions of their given schools of thought. Taking for immediate example the shifts and evolution in factional warfare that have taken place in the past five years, it was largely with the growth of radical feminism within the progressive political left and its "intersectional" identity politics that spurred the notable growth that the right and center-right have enjoyed. With many of a more liberal persuasion finding the shrill nonsense of outrage, offense and emotionally laden political hysteria a generally unacceptable evolution, voices from the conservative side of things began to appear more mature and sensible than they perhaps had in recent history.

Replacing the old panicky moral majority with its evangelicism and moral panics with a quippy, sarcastic tone and generally a more libertarian façade, the rise of the new right took place almost entirely upon the shoulders of the evolution of the new left. This new left being something that your author in this case has taken to calling "neoprogressivism." In this, through the simple act of pointing to the often garish and abrasive identity politics champions coming often directly out of schools and taking jobs as up-jumped bloggers who'd somehow managed to adopt the title of "journalist," those of a more conservative political and social persuasion found the substantially pliable attention of those who took to regarding such as garish and abrasive, often without holding much in the way of conservative conviction on their own. Painting themselves either as a sensible voice of reason in a time of utter madness, or at the very least a preferable alternative to the "social justice warriors," a new breed of Reaganite style youth with rather slight libertarian tinges, rose in overall prominence utilizing catchy phrases such as "facts don't care about your feelings," and even in some cases attempting to claim the mantel of liberalism while simultaneously praising the likes of Steve Bannon and Nigel Farage.

Not for anything generally considered robust defenses of actual liberalism, it was initially observed with the rise of the wannabe Oscar Wilde, Milo Yiannopoulos that the term "illiberal" was rightly, though pointedly used to describe the rise of the social justice phenomenon, bringing many who even considered themselves liberal to eagerly patron his various talks and media appearances, hoping if nothing else to hear some witty rebuttal of neoprogressive ideas. Yet laid within this, much in the fashion of the snarky, condescending liberalism of the 1990s, Yiannopoulos found great (albeit short lived) success in spreading his Thatcher-ite conservatism without the stuffiness typically associated with it. With a tone only slightly snarkier than that of Bill Maher, Yiannopoulos deftly tongue clicked and eye rolled his way to a place of political relevance utilizing a familiar mix of sensationalism, shock and blatant contrarianism.

Without even much in the way of genuine expression of support for the fundamental ideals Yiannopoulos stood for, legions of disaffected consumers of political banter took this brand of conservatism often singularly rooted in its aversion and hostility to the growing neo-progressive grievance culture movements observed in media and on college campuses. As many have since noted, this growth in "anti-social-justice" sentiment, which itself in many ways would eventually congeal into something vaguely resembling a cohesive ideology, did itself offer in roads for even more radical right wing figures to grow themselves. Serving as something of an opening act for what we would come to call the "alt-right," it was through the growing discontent with aggressive and authoritarian progressivism that many a race baiting nationalist with observable fascist sympathies were able to find their own fame and attention.

On the left this same observable growth in both the edgy condescending conservatism of people such as Yiannopoulos, Ben Shapiro or Sean Hannity, as well as even conspiracy theory dullards such as Alex Jones and Paul Joseph Watson, as well also of genuine white supremacists such as Richard Spencer fueled a radical reaction that pushed the left's own fringes even further into inanity. Growing beyond merely crying like children at the thought of a conservative voice being allowed to speak within mile of them, many on the more radical left began adopting hardline ideologies rooted in Marx, with the ever present smatterings of feminist and intersectional writers being strewn throughout. With many openly and proudly self-identifying as "queer communist revolutionaries" and other assorted progressive identity focused political nonsense terms, the generally unifying factor which came to spur on the growth of movements such as "Antifa" was the bitter hatred of anything considered conservative.

In a curious case of self-fulfilling prophecies, within the shrill din of bickering that took place in the years of 2013 through 2015, as social justice progressives took to calling any who opposed them Nazis and their anti-social justice counterparts claiming that the collegiate activists were nothing but communists, it wasn't really until 2016 or so that these terms actually came to describe active factions with the given camps. Within the political left socialist and communist sympathies have always been present. Likewise, within the broader political right fascistic and ethnic or cultural puritans have always existed. But it would largely seem that by virtue of volume and regularity on the part of combatants screaming that everyone on the opposite side of the proverbial fence is the embodiment of either Marxism or Nazism that the real Marxists and real Nazis have found their voices amplified in the course of the culture war.

The observable escalations of tension between the left and right as we've seen play out over the past several years offers an undeniable argument that the roots and nature of the ongoing culture war and conflagrations of political hostility are both cyclical and self nurturing. Rather than merely being chains of cause and effect, paradigms within the given sides are first observed by their detractors, made a point of mockery and scorn, then adopted, inflated, promoted and made into catalysts for another changing of hands.

Whereas detractors of perceived leftist progressivism once vocally derided identity politics, the foundations laid in that effort paved the way for grifters and frauds such as

Candace Owens or Laura Loomer to make careers utilizing and promoting an opposing and inverted identitarian victimhood narrative. Whereas detractors of perceived right wing racism previously railed endlessly against the divisions and derision of people over matters of race and sex, race and gender baiting hucksters such as Shaun King, or nearly any op-ed columnist from The Guardian to turn their own preferred forms of racism and sexism into supposed tools of social progress.

With the constantly evolving nature to these entrenched divisions and adoptions of sullied tactics, the escalation of such has gone hand in hand with each proverbial pendulum swing. As recently as 2014, the notion of political violence was something of a theoretical abstract to many observers. Enter 2016 however and the rise in both anti-fascist "Antifa" groups and the counter movements such as Patriot Prayer Group and The Proud Boys has created an environment where street brawls involving melee weapons and homemade explosives are almost a standard affair for partisan protests. In this it is not unreasonable to fear what comes next, with 20th century Europe offering us a frightening glimpse as to what it may be in the form of the years of lead.

For over a decade between the late 1960s and early 1980s, Europe – Italy in particular — were rocked by waves of escalating politically motivated violence and terrorism carried out by both left and right wing political factions. Rooted, much as our current American conflicts are now in the contest between right wing fascism and left wing communism, much of what took place during the *Anni di piombo* period was facilitated in a tit-for-tat fashion, with attacks against the perceived enemy launched and reprisals escalating with each given turn. It is not therefore altogether unreasonable to wonder that as the new ultra-nationalist right with their white supremacist factional allies and the neo-Marxist left with their anti-white and anti-male sentiments might not spin one another up into similar outbreaks of violence.

As it stands already, it was following the punching of Richard Spencer that the left found new wind in their sails as the slogan "punch a Nazi" or "bash the fash" came into fashion. Likewise in response to this, actual fascists began organizing around the assault citing how the left needed to be kept in check. This culminated eventually with the "Unite The Right" rally in Charlottesville, Virginia where in addition to tense standoffs and a number of assaults, progressive demonstrator Heather Heyer was killed when James Alex Fields Jr. drove his car into a dense street filled with protestors. As can and should be expected, Heyer became a martyr in the eyes of many and her death served as a call to many others to take up the mantel of Antifa, hence driving the matter even further forward into hostility and violence.

Growing as it has to become the new normal in respect to political activism, the factional violence itself, like any tribalist hostility feeds voraciously on its own perpetuation. Not merely in the sense that the standard cycles of violence which can be observed in most any violent conflict play out as one might expect, but also in that within many of the individuals taking part in their "protests," a sense of romantic righteousness is found in throwing a punch or swinging a club. Just as the masked protester who punched Richard Spencer following the inauguration of Donald Trump became something of an underground folk hero to many on the activist left, so too did the right see a rising violent star of their own in the form of Kyle Chapman, aka "Based Stick Man." Chapman rose to prominence in 2017 after being filmed beating an Antifa activist with a stick during a clash between pro and anti-Trump activists in Berkley California.

It wasn't long after Chapman's viral rise in popularity in the fringe right online that many a conservative "activist" would be found attending rallies and events, geared up and not only ready but eager for battle. In 2018, following his being invited to speak at a Proud Boys event in Massachusetts, Carl Benjamin (aka Sargon of Akkad) addressed a small crowd of anti-leftists, many of whom were sporting military helmets and armor. Though police were on site to maintain order and kept a wide berth between the event and the small bands of counter protestors who arrived, murmurs slithered throughout the small crowd over hopes that Antifa would show up and that another battle similar to those which took place in Berkeley and Portland might occur. In their voices, as my own recollection retains, there were not tones of concern or worry but rather an eager and active anticipation of what they'd hoped would transpire.

Beyond even this, another notable factor was how many within the crowd of perhaps two or three-dozen, would somewhat quietly identify themselves as actual fascists. Not to say it was a majority by any stretch of the imagination, their presence and the welcoming nature of those who sat to discuss how, if nothing else, fascism was preferable to the impending communist doom that many in attendance believed was approaching, offered a notable commentary as to how movements and counter movements attract some of the worst ideologues on offer. Perhaps more disconcerting then, being how they'll often tolerate them on the grounds that at least they're not the "other guys."

Naturally, though both sides in these given conflicts tend to blame the other either directly, citing some egregious deed done such as assault in the case of the various Antifa demonstrations or murder, such as in the case of Heather Heyer, or more generally citing some broader existential threat posed by the existence of their enemy's ideology, the underlying motivation on the part of individual combatants is often plainly obvious. This being, to acquire and possess the self-righteous thrill of participating in a pitched battle.. Ultimately , be it open political violence with the potential to get worse, or merely the incessant bickering and screeching refrains feeding into a perpetual shifting of snark and hysterics, the cyclical and self-sustaining nature of these generally insipid conflicts would suggest that nothing short of monumental calamity would serve as the necessary catalyst to halt or end these cycles of hostility.

Though these patterns can actually be traced back decades to times where the shifts and cycles moved slower, to note that with the advent of social media, viral videos and the often touted but rarely analyzed "new media" of YouTube and other streaming services, that such cycles have increased in speed and intensity, it can be easy to wonder if there is any hope of seeing an end or at least easing of such noise at all. However there does exist a sliver of hope in the observable trend evolving status quos. In this, though at any given time an ideology, movement, philosophy or trend may seem at the outset to be daring or rebellious (with many an established ideology and movement often seeking to adopt such a moniker intentionally) it doesn't take very long at all for popular political and cultural zeitgeists to become ingrained norms and themselves. The "rebels" of yesterday becoming the new status quo.

Beyond merely ascending to this level however out of the shadows of irrelevance and into the light of actual power, the churning and innate desire within primarily young people to reject the status quo regardless of what it might be serves as something of a bulwark against them becoming overly ingrained within society. Considering that teenage and young adult rebellion against what they see as stale and out of touch with the world they know is itself a double edged sword -as evidenced with the rise of both the hysterics of the far left and smarmy soft shoe racism of the far right- it remains a sound hope to consider what the rapidity of modern argument tends to be like in this respect. Whereas the slow moving waves of conservative and liberal dominance in the public dialogue of the past often forced change to be slow and protracted, it could at least be theorized that with a bit of luck, the next great rejection of establishment thinking will come not in the form of a partisan or ideological shift, but more an outright rejection of reactionary politics and the presumed value of the vocal pundit class.

If the next new trend or meme or take over as the next generation of young activists and keyboard warriors ascends to claim their place turns to be one wherein rational deliberation is held in higher esteem than being "woke" or "red pilled," we could perhaps see a short lived break in this otherwise inevitable and seemingly natural cycle. No longer, or at least for a time, would we as a society be subjected to the charlatanry and puerile chest thumping that presently dominates and defines our politics but instead, with a youthful and rebellious spirit, find the public dialectic returning to an interest in truth.

ESCAPING THE ECHO CHAMBER

An all too common accusation one is likely to hear a diehard ideologue accuse their opposition of is existing within an echo chamber. For those not immediately familiar with the term, it refers to an environment wherein only agreeable positions or opinions are made available. It typically tends to be applied (rightly) to the more progressive universities in the US and UK where speakers are disinvited, banned, barred and deplatformed after student activist groups and activist faculty express grave fear and concern over the speakers tone, tenor or ideas.

Though these ideas themselves are typically as innocuous as raising the question as to whether political correctness and hyper-sensitivity are in fact harmful to students and destructive in a free society, they nevertheless find themselves proven quite thoroughly in the screeching demands by students and activists to banish the very thought itself. A central aspect and element to the unfortunate nature of social media as it relates to this very matter, is the nature of bans, blocks and bubbles as they form within social media feeds and communities. Within this the banishing of those who oppose given ideas as posited by online slacktivists is itself a means by which such groups seek to protect their generally vulnerable and fragile ideologies by ensuring nary a word in opposition can be uttered in their presence.

Echo chambers are not limited to the regressive left, even if they have more traditionally found their home there in recent times. A great number of pro-Trump, pro-GOP and pro-ethnostate groups and discussion forums online routinely purge what they regard as wrongthink, citing as their counterparts on the left often do, the need to "keep the trolls out." It is an easily identifiable marker of an insulated echo chamber when dissent, criticism or argument is met with the immediate defining of those offering such as "trolls."

These insular environments and conversations are themselves rather central in the advancing of radical or fringe ideas, but are also equally essential in the maintaining of the generally frantic division and hostility. After all, one's ideas can never be changed or challenged if no challenge is ever allowed near them. Yet beyond this there exists the nature of hyper-charging of ideology through what for lack of a better term is dubbed an ideological circle jerk. With validations abounding on all sides and nary a contrary voice to be heard, these environments – ranging from Facebook groups and pages to campus political organizations – are such where gross villainizing of perceived opposition goes equally unchallenged, building layer upon layer until any to the right of Mao are deemed Nazis and any to the left of Pinochet denounced as Stalinists.

Again, tapping on the previously illustrated nature of these presumptions often fueling the actual rise of such caricatures to places of actual albeit marginal relevance, it becomes easier to observe the processes by which radical fringes and even more basic ideologues tend to feed off of one another. With the concept of "when they start shooting at you, you're doing something right" taken to a more pathetic and pedantic place, it is from within the echo chambers that the true believer finds every ounce of opposition ranging from run of the mill argument to standard shit talking and insult to appear like bullets hurtling at them in a desperate attempt to stop them and their entirely valid ideology from saving the world from the communists, Nazis, Islamists, liberals, conservatives and so on.

Now to be certain, such environments do not always form up for the exclusive purposes of being ideologically or philosophically exclusive. More often than not, regardless of their focus, pages, groups and various other forms of association, be they in the real world or online, begin as places for common interests. Are you a liberally minded person with a progressive political attitude who wishes to discuss such matters with others of a similar mind? Well this group right here might be just perfect for you. Are you a conservative who wishes to discuss traditional values, national pride or any of the other standard canon items associated with the term? Likewise, there exists a litany of groups of likeminded people waiting for you. So on and so forth.

However much as the inspiration of an ideal can bring people together, so too can a bitter hatred of an 'other.' Looking again to the cyclical notion of hostility, just as perceived and real fascists can drive many harder left and the real and perceived cultural authoritarian streaks on the left can likewise drive others harder right, the draw and pull of many of these groups and pages and forums can be less about the dedicated support and enthusiasm for a set of beliefs as much as a deep rooted disdain for something else. Rather than seeking a place to discuss social welfare, traditional values, policy reform or taxation, many seek out such environments for a place to opine, guffaw and bluster at the dire idiocy perceived from the other side.

Prior to landing a book deal, my first paid writing job actually came by way of one of these very sorts of groups. Started as merely a Facebook page dedicated to trash talking the Tea Party of the early 2010s, "Americans Against The Tea Party" (AATTP) soon launched a dedicated news aggregation website designed for this very same purpose. Taking up the styling of clickbait websites that had come before such as Upworthy and Buzzfeed, AATTP relied on home based writers to read already reported upon news stories, find those which specifically made anything and anyone branded as right wing look bad and then play up those elements in a pointed re-write of the story itself.

Brought on board initially after an editor read a lengthy comment I'd left on an article somewhere on social media (with lengthy comments having been something I was once known for when I used social media more regularly) I was first invited to write for a sister site known as AtlasLeft. Here I was told I would be free to write about whatever I wished, with a humble payment coming through based on the clicks an article received. Yet before I was even able to write a piece for this site, I found myself immediately traded over to AATTP with flurries of politically charged op-eds and news reports thrown at me daily for the expressed purpose of retooling them into partisan hit pieces.

When sent an article about a tragic accident involving a toddler killing their sibling upon finding their father's unsecured handgun, despite my re-writing of the facts of the case as I could find them, with deeper digging being performed via local news reports in the hopes of discovering new information, the grim and factual article I provided was rapidly edited and branded with the obnoxious title "Toddler 2nd Amendments Sibling, NRA Cheers." When forwarded the story of a mentally ill man from the Midwest who, while wearing actual tinfoil on his head, burned his house down, blamed then President Obama and was arrested with firearms, despite there being no political connection to be made aside from the conspiratorial ramblings of a sick individual, AATTP took delight in reframing my article to read as though this man was emblematic of conservatives and gun owners. In fact, so sloppy and eager to fire off generally bogus interpretations of stories, so as to stir the partisan pot, AATTP would frequently overlook the fact that the original sources for many of the articles they sought to aggregate where themselves highly suspect if not outright dubious to begin with.

The point here being however that within the chest thumping partisan fervor of such closed systems as AATTP, who routinely booted commenters or page visitors for challenging stated beliefs, the self-sustaining fervor and enthusiasm for engaging in battles of snark and derision was on full and perfect display. Here, not only were guests and visitors encouraged partake in believing that gun owners cheered when children shot one another, but writers were encouraged and sometimes even ordered to frame matters in such ways. To be sure the monetary motivations helped quite a bit, yet it was within the horrendous glee with which the senior staff perpetuated such horrendous garbage that really serves to outline just how the ecology of insulated outrage works.

Thankfully I was able to break with this organization after only a few short weeks of writing for them and soon found a more idea-focused publisher almost immediately, however as I was myself rather new to such things in general, even in this I found the differences between an open idea-focused editorial board and those of my previously foul and directed guidelines to be like night and day. Whereas previously I was told what to write and how to write it, I was not free to select, investigate and report upon stories I felt mattered. Sadly though, even as site administrators, publication editors and the social media presence itself was one of the open sharing of reports, ideas and perspectives, the environment that formed up within it was not always so kind. Death threats it seems, are far from limited to the fringe right. A reality I came face to face within a relatively short order.

In 2016, still writing part time for the activist website Occupy.com, I penned an article addressing the new and rising tides of the violent and chaotic "Antifa" movement. In it, I begged those of a liberal or progressive persuasion not to support or condone the violence and destruction the masked anarchists touted as their activism and called for a restoration of the traditional liberal ideals of mature conversation and deliberation. Upon being posted to Facebook by my friend, the satirist Vermin Supreme, accusations ranged from me being an undercover police officer or federal agent looking to undermine a movement, to my being a suspected fascist infiltrator. Comments stating how I should be looked into and should catch a bullet became common and the accusations about my being law enforcement continued in pitch and din until Vermin himself commented stating that I was most certainly not a cop.

And even still, this would not be my final personal encounter with an echo chamber prior to the writing of this book. At about the same time I penned my article entitled "Letter To The American Left," I was myself in the midst of what we can now call the early days of this modern cultural conflict. A friend to many an "anti-feminist" or "anti-sjw" YouTuber, I began noting in the early days of 2016 that the conversations both between content creators and with their fans and subscribers, became rather stale and repetitive. Not only where refrains about the dangers and evils of social justice progressivism recited almost verbatim between different parties, but the conversations as a whole seemed in many instances to focus almost exclusively upon such, with little in the way of even mild and polite small talk occurring between anyone. It was at about this time that the notion of everything looking like a nail when all you have is a hammer began to take on a new life and meaning for me.

As time went on and small pittances of support from places like Patreon and Google rolled in, the broader world around me seemed increasingly to focus on and be framed in the colors of culture war. Behind every piece of art, entertainment, within the casting of any film or tv show and even within corporate ad campaigns, shades of social justice versus what at the time was erroneously dubbed "skepticism" could be found. This isn't to say they could be observed as much as specifically found, when one sought to see them.

In much the same way that my now largely former colleagues and I used to mock and deride the hysterical feminist radicals who saw rape and patriarchy in just about anything, it seemed that many a "red pilled" writer or YouTuber began seeing the signs of a sneaking and subversive progressive or even communist agenda lurking around every corner. While I count myself largely fortunate to have broken mostly free of this habit of seeking out windmills to tilt at, many others did not, be it for ideological or professional reasons. Instead, while remaining wholly mired in this culture war mentality and keeping largely to fraternizing with those of similar factional and ideological leanings, many who had previously or still maintain a mantel of liberalism or being politically left of center have taken to vocally supporting parties such as

Donald Trump, Steve Bannon, conspiracy theory mouth breathers like Alex Jones or even phony conservative charlatans such as Candace Owens and Dave Rubin.

While many openly claim they support such figures because of how they "trigger the left," many others after prolonged immersion in this culture war mentality have found whatever dogmatic messaging espoused by these players to be amenable to their own perceived liberalism. In some more extreme cases, some previously claiming to embrace liberal or progressive sentiments while opposing the neo-progressive hysteria of identity politics have even taken to crackpot theories such as "race realism," which asserts that intelligence is racially influenced with some races just being naturally genetically more intelligent than others. Yet beyond even the simple and tragic matter of ideologues being themselves forged in the fires of echo chamber rhetoric, there exists likewise the inverse effect upon those who run afoul of the status-quo or come into conflict with that which is accepted doctrine within a given community.

For one example of such, we can look to the pairing of Joseph Lancaster (aka Kraut and Tea) and David Sherrat (formerly known as Spinosauruskin.) With both of these individuals, their online presence as commentators on social and political affairs began with anti-feminism and promotion of men's rights. As they each rose in respective profiles this soon expanded to opposing the broader social justice phenomenon and radical Islam. However following a disastrous effort to combat the growing ranks of the Alt-right, both fell deeply out of favor with many who occupied the anti-feminist, anti-sjw circles generally regarded as the "skeptic community." Quickly allying themselves with many of the same people they once viciously derided for their social justice ideologies, the pair quickly found themselves as warmly embraced by their former nemeses as they were mercilessly attacked by their former friends and allies.

And yet again, even within that simple statement the notion of enemies and allies reinforced by the closed systems of ideological alliances which open up communications with their adversaries typically for the sole purpose of participating in some perceived concept of battle is again reaffirmed. Not even merely existing as fortresses for the faithful to gather together and work against their foes, one's very place within what are otherwise typically regarded publicly as social circles of friends hinges quite often on one's willingness to acquiesce to and promote the common zeitgeist of "us" and "them." A curious, organic system, which on its own, regardless of ideological focus, seems to have created the very sorts of political purity tests that the twentieth century authoritarian movements of both left and right often dreamed of.

But for all this exploration and consideration of what an echo chamber is, what of the means of escape? Where in this particular diatribe will we find the path and keys to the fire exit, so as to leave the chamber and breathe easy in the open air? While some might suggest a calm and measured immersion in what the "other side" is up to, I would, for my part, suggest going a step further.

In much the same way that social media helps create these enclosures for simple agreement and can fundamentally alter the underlying nature to social interaction, separating one's self entirely from it, even if for a short time, can be invaluable in terms of perspective. In this, while attempting to "take a break" from participating in the campaigns, crusades, attacks and memes of a given side can offer some clarity in respect to the collection and collation of such thinking, taking a break from thinking about such at all can be infinitely more effective. As I've been fond of saying in bored response to many an insipid hot take, 'get a new hobby.'

Binge watch a television show and ignore the politics of the writers or actors or director. Read a good book that has nothing to do with left or right. Spend time with friends and make a point to avoid raising the topics of social politics, not for any sense of good manners, but rather simply to break yourself of the habits of doing so.

Upon many a public meet-up with fellow YouTube creators and local fans, attempts to discuss matters other than social politics can be found to be difficult, as even a simple conversation about beer or literature will often be skewed in the direction of culture war concerns by simple sustained interest on the part of attending fans. Though initially finding such a grating inevitability, I soon found it to be itself a form of commentary serving as a reminder of just how deep the roots of such mentalities can reach and how difficult it can be, once mired, to extract one's self even for a simple evening of drinks and friendly company.

To those who live for competing outrages, partisan contests, ideological feuds and political crusades, I can only in the strongest terms encourage this; swear it off for at least two weeks. Rid yourself of the instinct or compulsion to respond to or comment on the routine churning of hot topics and hotter takes. Struggle with it as you must, but carve out a mental vacation, even if it means ignoring social media and the internet altogether. Remove yourself from the battlefield and look not upon it until the ease with which you ignore it rises to the level of simple breathing.

Then upon successfully extracting yourself, look back upon it with eyes as attuned as possible to just pretending it is all new to you. Become the stranger in a once familiar land and ask if beyond the often petty reactions and responses hurled in either direction, if it resembles the same monumental struggle you may have previously regarded it to be. Ask yourself if your efforts or attention were perhaps in vain and seek out the cycles of perpetuation as they exist, not within the issues under discussion, but within the cultures attempting to champion their given sides.

If you do not find yourself free of the weight and burdens of being a foot soldier in the culture war, you may at the very least notice marked similarities in the way things operate between feuding parties and maybe, with a bit of luck, may find yourself wholly liberated of your own insular environment in a way that might allow for a calmer and more objective look at matters as they are presented. This is itself not a call to adopt a centrist mentality as no manner of thought is worth a damn if adopted as a trend or at the request of another, but rather if nothing else, is offering up an opportunity for a bit of mental decompression, which in an age of echo chambers and pitched ideological battles, is a rare and precious thing unto itself.

THE LOST VIRTUE OF ART

Throughout human history, little has offered man the ability to reflect upon the world around him as effectively as art. Through music, theater, the written word or the painted image, art and artistic expression have served to not only express the desires, fears, hopes, observations and imaginings of human beings, but to build a repository of such which allows us to look back with considerate eyes and compare and contrast our present with our past. It is not much of a stretch to say that in respect to something as fundamental as love itself, it is largely though the arts that many if not most of us have come to learn to romanticize the romantic.

To say as well that through our varied mediums of artistic expression, we have for generations now continually critiqued and refined our understandings of matters political and cultural in nature, it becomes nearly impossible to deny the central and crucial role the arts have played in the shaping of our numerous and varied societies worldwide. So crucial, that in many a revolution or sudden revolt, control of not just the general media such as television and radio news broadcasts, but control of the arts themselves is essential for establishing and maintaining a grip on the culture's psyche. Is it any wonder that more authoritarian regimes such as China, Cuba or the majority of the Islamic world maintain tight restrictions on what can be expressed and how?

Yet restrictive authoritarianism isn't limited to strong arm governments and state ideologies. A look throughout even the freest of liberal democracies will often turn up regular internal conflicts between factions of left and right for control of the arts, highlighting in stark relief their central importance to popular deliberations. In these conflicts, we see as we do in the routine battles fought over matters of public policy, a defined effort either by one side or another, to use generally socially borne political pressures to mold and control various mediums. However, within them more directly, we also see the often inevitable changing of hands in respect to whom it is that seeks to be the censor of the day.

Just as more conventional conservative evangelicals and social conservatives throughout the twentieth century often sought to curtail and growth of a lot of the more avant-garde or daring artists, writers and musicians, frequently regarding their work as "anti-American," "anti-Christian" or simply dangerous to what they understood to be the social fabric of our society, things, as they often do, have changed hands more recently, with the heirs to their moral panics now attempting a similar effort, albeit for much different means.

Stretching as far back as the nineteen-twenties, traditionalist conservatism, which at the time still held tightly to the notions of segregation, has routinely stood in opposition to art and media they find to run contrary to their ideals. In the twenties, as jazz offered the youth of the age not only the stepping stones to racial integration (a serious issue of concern for white America at the time) but also a more foot-loose and fancy-free scene in which to revel and rebel, the genre became so routinely attacked by its detractors that such was even incorporated into the 1936 film *Reefer Madness*, where black and brown jazz musicians were portrayed as violent rapists, triggered into assaults by the madness brought about by marijuana. Skip forward then into the 1960's and 70's, where the spiritual successors to the beatnicks of old, the hippies, with their free love and jam band grooves, triggered another surge of middle American moral panic, insisting that the evolving genre of rock music was influencing and corrupting the youth. Those of a harder line nationalistic conservatism even often took to bashing the music of the anti-war movement as being subversive and dangerous.

Tracking this even further, we can look to the moral panics of the Reagan and Bush eras where heavy metals music, rap, hip-hop and other genres which would reflect upon or espouse anti-Christian or anti-state messages were such targets of these self proclaimed moral authorities, that such lead to congressional hearings and legally mandated parental advisories. Yet these considerations are not even meant in this particular context, to highlight the authoritarian nature to twentieth century conservatism – an aspect to such generally overlooked amid the right's recent resurgence as a libertarian counter-culture — but more to highlight and emphasize that despite their best efforts, the laissez-faire nature to our culture, which is so often expressed in our art and music, won the day regardless.

Consider for a moment the state of modern music. There is very little that can be said, or sung, or painted, or represented in film, or described in literature, which can really shock us short of short term matters of personal or political offense. The gangsta rap of the 90s, cited often by moral puritans as being incitements to violence, pale in comparison to what many satirical or alternately black metal music lyrics and tones can be found on offer today. Found, I should add, to have far less a scintillating nature, while also being in many cases far more graphic, violent or conventionally offensive.

However it is thus that we come to find the newest breed of authoritarian busy-bodies seeking to control the flow and content of art which challenges their world views. Just as the stodgy old social conservatism of the twentieth century has largely gone the way of disco, the new moral authorities are those coming largely from the left as part of its wave of social justice purists. Whereas purists of old would cite graphic violence in film or television, or it's depiction in music as dangerous to children, many a modern aspiring censor decries such on the grounds of its chances of emotionally triggering themselves or their peers, many of whom are in their twenties or thirties.

If not rooting their opposition to art or artists in some straining effort to protect themselves or their friends from the presumed trauma that a fictional representation of a terrible event, or alternately the mere uttering of a word they don't like might be, they go a step farther, insisting that they and their ilk act as watchdogs for ethnic, sexual or ideological minorities, demanding that at no time should anything that could be perceived as offensive to them, ever see the light of day. Beyond this though, they even go another step further, weaponizing the notion of "deplatforming" whenever an artist, presenter or creator is found to, at any time in their lives, have expressed a view or made a joke that failed to respect these very general principles.

Yet even prior to the drum beat of the modern outrage culture citing often obscure elements within art deemed to be grossly offensive to this group or that, the most common grievance with the artistic world is generally that of representation. Should a film, book, video game or television show lack the levels of diversity expected by campaigners, it is often slammed as being some form of exclusionary, biased or "phobic," simply for not presenting classes, cultures, races, creeds, genders and sexualities as those who are not even part of an intended audience demand. This sort of inclusion lunacy has even gone so far as to insist upon racial diversity in ancient or historical settings, in which such diversity did not actually exist. In this, we're offered the next step in irrational crusades against art wherein demands are made to literally rewrite history as a means to appease those who believe such is necessary for promoting a just and equitable society.

In this modern shift however, wherein art and media has increasingly become not merely a central battleground for cultural crusaders, but in some cases *the* central battleground, the notion of tactics and strategies as well as philosophies and justifications changing hands seems to have taken on an even more direct and more aggressive pace. For it was largely within the first five or so years of this, the second decade of the twenty-first century, that we really saw the first serious volleys against our entertainment media made in this modern fight. To be sure, the Reaganites of the 80s attacked rap and hard rock and the feminists of the 1990s attacked nearly anything with a male lead. Yet it was in the opening of the twenty-teens when within this new media environment of YouTube, Facebook and Twitter that we began seeing more concerted efforts by those such as Anita Sarkeesian, which sought to inject intersectional feminism and social justice politics into everything, including video games.

As the fight over video games lead into what would later be called "Gamergate" throughout 2014, 2015 and into 2016, the levels of sniping between campaigners on both sides to out the speakers, artists and critics on the other side to be sinister sex pests, racists, misogynists, misandrists and so on escalated to a point where the simple and innocent outsider perspective by said artists could and often did wind up branding them the "enemy" of a given movement. In this, many who stood against the politically correct, intersectionalist movements found themselves bothered and conflicted when creators of fiction that they love, such as Joss Whedon, came out staunchly and proudly as allies to the progressives. A similar matter occurred when the chattering classes would discover alternately that a creator, writer or director they admired, or in the case of video games, a developer, would express an opinion or even make a joke, that riled the outrage of the neo-progressive mobs, causing further internal conflict as to the value of a piece of art versus the politics of the artist in question.

These divisions deepened further as subsequent events over just a few years continued to evolve. With the neo-progressive movement of identitarians wages vocal and sometimes effective campaigns to deplatform, boycott and shame artists for their political opinions, it didn't take long for elements in the right to pick this same tactic up and put it to work. In 2018, as director James Gunn was enjoying massive successes helming the Guardians of The Galaxy film series, it was after his taking and expressing a staunchly anti-Trump stance that conservative writer Mike Cernovich decided to dredge up a series of years old tweets by Gunn wherein he made several off color pedophilia jokes and effectively end his tenure heading one of Marvel Studio's most successful franchises. Despite being Cernovich being himself celebrated by many on the right as a free speech champion, while Cernovich himself and many a follower of his had previously spent years complaining about such a dirty tactic being used by the progressive left, many a defender stood up to cheer for the dullard writer commonly referred to as "Juicebro," stating that it was time to "teach the left a lesson."

Not to be confused however, even in spite of the widespread controversy surrounding the implementation of this deplatforming tactic of using years old social media comments or jokes to tar and feather an artist of different politics than one's self, progressives opted to again deploy such later that year, demanding that comedian Kevin Hart be stripped of his invitation to host the Academy Awards after statements deemed "homophobic" were dredged up from a year's old comedy routine of his. This same matter also played a part in the downfall of comic legend Louis C.K., when campaigners discovered to their shock that a man who built a career joking about his romantic and sexual inadequacy and who frequently told joking stories about his almost pathological behavior, was outed for exposing himself and masturbating in front of female comedians repeatedly throughout the years. Without defending his actions, the common knowledge of comics often being impulsive, neurotic and altogether damaged people seemed as overlooked as the years and years of very dark and twisted reflections of his thinking that went into his comedy altogether. In essence, anyone who was stunned to learn that Louis C.K. is and was a disturbed sex pest clearly never listened to his act.

In Louie's case, we the public, were treated to a second round when in the midst of an attempted comeback, leaked audio of a generally unrefined stand up set he was working on outraged members in the progressive public sphere when a line or two joking about school shooting survivors made it clear to anyone familiar with his work that those who were upset were themselves, not familiar in the slightest.

Throughout all of this though, the back and forth of

attempts to control and cajole the creators of our media to abide by various puritanical strings of traditional or progressive political thought, the adoption of wretched tactics by those who may have previously lambasted them as underhanded and unacceptable, the insistence that art reflect not the values or thoughts of the creator, but those of a potential audience, all of this ultimately falls largely flat when the central question is raised; "Is it correct to judge a piece of art or media by the politics held by the artist?"

For perhaps the most to-the-point instance, we need look no farther than everyone's favorite political boogey man, Adolph Hitler. While it takes a particular breed of stupidity to defend Hitler's politics or legacy, to look to his paintings and the artistic talent displayed within them, one will find, if honest, something of a bothersome divergence in thinking. One who was arguably one of the most vile and evil dictators to ever grace the west, it feels wrong and difficult for most to separate this consideration from that of his art as despite his wicked and unspeakably evil nature, his paintings were surprisingly good.

But perhaps jumping straight to Hitler, a favorite tactic of most diehard ideologues at one time or another, may be a bit too on the nose for such a line of thinking as this. Instead then, let's consider an American icon in the world of poetry. A man whose work is, to one extent or another, in some way familiar to nearly anyone with a moderate level of education. To recite the lines "I saw the best minds of my generation destroyed by madness, starving hysterical naked," to nearly anyone with some familiarity with English literature or poetry, is a bit like reciting the first line of the Declaration of Independence to a first year civics student.

Allen Ginsberg, author of the poem "Howl" is often regarded by most with interests in literature to be one of the premiere American poets of the 20th century. Showered with awards and accolades throughout his career, many to this day regard Ginsberg to be the voice of the beat generation. Yet in spite of this, what is lesser known about the National Book Award winner is that he was also a vocal advocate for pedophilia.

This was something that even I, a lover of literature and history, was only made aware of last year, when after reciting the entirety of "Howl" for a YouTube video on my channel, Wizard of Cause, I was alerted to the grim fact in the comment section. It was upon this enlightenment as to the poet's nefarious predilections though, that I first sought to weigh and balance out the value of a piece of art when held in the shadow of its artists' darker nature. It was then that the truest questioning of art versus artist and the necessity and risk of separating one from the other really began churning about in my mind.

Having been inundated in the culture war from its earliest days, finding the grating calls of activists who lobbed often silly and pointless inflections of the ideological expectations upon seemingly everything, I did for a while find myself increasingly adopting such knee-jerk reactions myself. Where I to learn, from my generally left leaning centrism, that the creator of a comic, the author of a book, an actor, director or musician, held views I deemed to be extreme or more plainly, just wrong, I noticed it began grating on me in my attempts to enjoy their creations. As a long time fan of Blackstar, the hip-hop duo of Mos Def and Talib Kweli, it pained me to see via social media, the staunch and sometimes inane identitarianism expressed respectively between the two, with Kweli taking generally more extreme stances than those of Mos Def. Likewise, a longtime fan of author Neil Gaiman, I found his promotion of a rather radical and misandrist feminists such as Randy Lee Harper (a notorious scam artist, doxer and online bully) dismaying, hoping that such a genius author would be wise enough to see through the veneer of righteousness that is so common to people such as Harper.

Ultimately however, after a notable stretch of reflection on the issue, it occurred to me that just as my own political opinions would undoubtedly rustle the feathers of any number of potential readers or audience members, that I was in no real place to judge in respect to how I viewed the art created by the artists in question. Not to be exclusively anti-left in this respect, an anecdote I'm fond of recounting in certain company recalls a time on Twitter wherein actors Adam Baldwin of Firefly fame and James Woods, famous for 'take-your-pick,' teamed up to berate me as an anti-American communist for suggesting that the intelligence operations to remove Mohammed Mossadegh from power in Iran in the 1950s was a catalyst for the hostilities the U.S. grapples with presently in Persia. Though a not altogether bombastic analysis on my part, it was after this online berating and subsequent blocking by the two actors, both of whom I'm a fan of, that I was forced to reassess the impact of an individual's politics on the manner in which I enjoy their work.

Should I cease to enjoy American Gods, my favorite novel of all time, simply because Neil Gaiman's personal politics throws support to known bad actors? Should I cease to enjoy Firefly because it stars a chest thumping neo-conservative, while being directed by an intersectional feminist? Ought I weigh the value of media, art and entertainment, which has otherwise been not only supremely enjoyable but in many cases, inspirational in the course of my own creative endeavors, against the politics held by the artist in question?

Is it right to look at a painting by Adolph Hitler and judge the artistic merits of the piece itself by the unrelated politics of its creator? Do his landscapes appear shadowy or ill crafted by virtue of his evil deeds, or is there perhaps even greater appreciation to be found in separating the two from the start? As with most questions of such a sort, there likely exists no clear answer outside of the opinion of the individual being asked, but for my part, I would say that separation of art and artist in such a fashion is not only healthy for our considerations of art in general, but fundamental to our ability to compartmentalize competing questions in ways that allow us greater understanding of their meaning altogether.

The politicization of art and creative expression is not something we can simply do away with, as it is in many cases something we cannot do without. With a great deal of art being itself political or culturally critical in nature, the underlying intent, be it obvious or belied, must be recognized and considered within the context of its relevance and presentation. Yet so long as individuals pour obsessively over the politics of an artist in an attempt to divine a deeper opinion about the art they love, the expressive value to such is diminished with every passing second of such consideration.

Likewise in respect to art that is meant to convey a political or cultural critique of some kind, with so much of it being expressed in vague and interpretable terms, the rushes to judgment on the part of so many watching can likewise diffuse the impact and calls to discussion such pieces of creation may fundamentally be about inspiring in the first place. Couple this then with the fact that a great deal of our media, art and entertainment is actually meant to be a-political in nature, the eagerness of many to read too far into such, whether through extractions of presumed meaning from the piece itself or through the filtering of consideration of it via analyses of the presumed politics of the artist, fundamentally serves more to spoil creativity than to offer it any real substance.

Like all other things, the centrally invaluable mediums of our artistic and creative expressions find themselves routinely under threat and assault from the orthodoxies and the demands of ideological devotion. Whether it be a matter of attempting to weaponize and propagandize using a piece of fiction, or the attempts to destroy the works and careers of artists with whom some have disagreements, the fundamental importance of art is all too often forgotten beneath the ceaseless din of partisan enthusiasm. And throughout this, all the while, there is no telling how many bold, mind changing expressions or abstractions may go un-created, simply by virtue of the voice and volume of those whose lives are dedicated to tearing down, disabusing and de-platforming those of talent and craft.

Ultimately, it is important not to lose sight of what is most fundamental in respect to the value and virtue of art. Beyond merely being expressive, it is at its core transcendent as well. Serving when it can as both a commentary and a record of concepts, thoughts and events, it also exists within our minds and societies as something which can be at any moment fully above and beyond the sometimes petty or trivial concerns of the real world. Allowing us a reprieve from the doldrums of conflict or care, even when focusing upon it, art, music, the written word and the spoken line beg us not only to be reflective in our considerations, but in equal measure, to set them aside entirely and indulge in the persistent reality that beauty exists in addition to and often in defiance of whatever sullied trivialities of the day may be pressing.

COMEDY GATEKEEPERS

Whereas expressive mediums such as theater, film, literature and music all can and often do serve as somewhat on-the-nose commentaries on the state of the world around us, few creative expressions can be as biting and poignant as comedy. Beyond satirical criticism or the open lampooning of sitting elected officials, news stories and the pressing goings on of a given day, comedy also allows for something of a decompression and assistance in compartmentalization of events, tragedies and public personalities. In this, by taking a joking and humorous approach to matters that are otherwise dark or distressing, our rational minds are offered the chance to take a break from dwelling emotionally within our reactions to things and defuse the tension that certain topics create. The dual benefit being that in addition to taking a break from the intense and sometime blinding reactions we're all naturally prone to, when one returns to offering serious consideration of a topic, event, figure or question, they can do so with hopefully a greater level of calm and poise in the process.

But beyond these simple benefits and the underlying reality that simply having a laugh, be it over a serious matter taken on jokingly or just a good punchline to an otherwise innocuous joke, comedy allows for a special sort of critical analysis. Though I generally loathe citing him, one of Jordon Peterson's more notable go-to allegories in respect to his views on free speech actually centers on the nature of the comedian as a civic actor. Noting that in feudal times when kings ruled over their nations with unquestionable power, that criticism of a sitting monarch or their dynasty was honestly only possible or allowed when spoken from the lips of the fool.

Not to say just any fool, but the court jester in this respect was, as Peterson puts it, the only party who could level criticism of a monarch without an automatic fear of reprisal. This being naturally because any such criticisms would be veiled in humor, taking what would be an offense that could warrant a death penalty and presenting it in a manner that the king and his court would not only forgive, but (provided the joke landed) enjoy. This same truth exists even today, wherein racy stand up comedians, cartoonists and sketch performers are often the only parties who raise certain points or criticisms without undue fear of public reprisals.

At least, some of the time.

To be sure, throughout ancient history a jester or two or three were most certainly beheaded, drawn and quartered or locked away in some dank dungeon for the crime of offending his or her majesty with a bit, skit or joke. Likewise throughout even the twentieth century, comics who sought to push the envelope found themselves on the receiving end of some rather harsh treatment. Throughout the 1960s comedian Lenny Bruce was repeatedly arrested for violation of obscenity laws in California, Illinois and New York and was expelled from England following a show in London.

Yet though to many Bruce is remembered firstly as a

comedian, to many others the name Lenny Bruce is itself more synonymous with free speech than any of the bits or jokes which landed him in such hot water. During his trial and subsequent conviction following an arrest in New York in 1964, a coalition of artists including Bob Dylan, Norman Mailer and even the previously mentioned poet Allen Ginsberg submitted a petition calling on the court to exonerate Bruce stating that he "should be allowed to perform free from censorship or harassment." This trial and conviction itself served in its time as something of a rallying cry for artists, writers and comedians who felt it was their duty as artists to defend free expression in the arts. Among many other twentieth century comedians who are often hailed as equally if not more so for their contributions in the fight to defend free expression, we were also graced with the likes of George Carlin, Bill Hicks and Sam Kinison, each of whom pushed the boundaries of what was considered "in good taste" while also offering some very long lasting perspectives on the myriads of topics they joked about.

More modernly a wide range of stand-up comics still often make their careers pushing the envelope, such as Anthony Jeselnik, who is generally noted for abandoning the conventional notion of a time being "too soon" to joke about a national tragedy, making cracks on Twitter and incorporating said jokes into his act sometime immediately after they take place. Within the catalog of Jeselnik's outrage courting, jokes made about the Boston Marathon bombing of 2013 the day of the attacks stirred considerable controversy around the comic, causing serious and contentious rows between he and the producers at Comedy Central, where his show The Jeselnik Offensive aired for two seasons. But not all matters of outrage in our modern age, wherein to many the notion of free speech is a settled fact, stem from conventional puritanism of the sorts which went after Bruce, Kinison or Hicks.

As described earlier, the shifting and trading of roles and methodologies between the political left and right has caused a modern uptick in more progressive outrages, with jokes, skits, acts or bits that could be perceived to be racist, sexist, transphobic or just generally insensitive causing comedians and comic writers to be on defensive as the modern day outrage mobs descend at venue after venue. With comics like Jerry Seinfeld and Chris Rock openly stating that they won't play modern college campuses due to the hyper-sensitivity on the part of many students, comedy itself has become yet another front on which the culture war and the fight for free expression are being waged.

Partially rooted in the new puritanical neo-progressive movement, wherein all identities, senses of identity and sensitivity to these are held in substantially higher regard than the concept of basic human rights such as that of free expression, the modern assaults on comedic expression are also very much the continuation of a pattern of bad activism. Having attacked literature, science fiction, the music industry, the film world, comic books and of course video games, many modern day campaigners have turned their sights on the world of comedy, demanding that it conform to the new zeitgeist of mandated inclusivity, diversity and sensitivity. Naturally however, comedians are pushing back.

If there is one type of artist or creator in the world of artistic expression that one is best not to hassle with demands that they change their work, it's the stand up comic. Not only is a good comic ideally prepared for and experienced with the arrival of a heckler in their audience, they also typically rely almost entirely on a biting and often acerbic wit, not only to deal with such pests, but as a basic and fundamental lens through which they see the world. In short, activists will generally if not always ultimately fail when trying to argue with a comedian. One could even say that even attempting such is both futile and ultimately stupid, as if a comic is worth their salt at all, they're not only ready to respond, but will likely bury whatever fuming outrage their confronted with beneath the laughter of those around to hear it.

Yet all the same, the assaults on comedy are not limited to the screechings of offended college students. In 2016, my own friend, Scottish YouTuber Markus Meecham, going by the online name "Count Dankula" produced a short video wherein for the explicit purpose of annoying his girlfriend, Meecham trained their pug "Buddha" to respond to the term "gas the Jews" and present a Nazi salute for a video he posted to YouTube. Being subsequently arrested for "hatespeech," he became internationally known as his trial proceeded to drag out for two years, with Meecham insisting upon his innocence every step of the way.

In conversations with him, Meecham routinely doubled down on the insistence that his joke was harmless, even quipping that in the very use of a pug for the joke, a dog whose breed suffers from regular health and breathing problems as a result of the breeding efforts which created them, serves as an excellent demonstration of how wrong the Nazi ideology is. Stating that nothing was a better example of what a bad idea it is for man to play god, Meecham, who regularly uses Buddha in videos even today, is steadfast in his convictions that not only ought comedy be a protected form of free speech, but that ultimately his joke, while harmless, also presents a more staunch position against Nazism than those espoused by so many left leaning activists.

Ultimately, despite arguing (quite correctly) that

context does in fact matter in relation to the uttering of statements and that hatespeech laws themselves are generally more harmful to a society than the speech they seek to police, Meecham was convicted in 2018 and sentenced to pay an £800 fine. Though he was facing the potential for up to a year in prison, it is generally assumed by many that the fine was levied so as to avoid making a martyr of the man whose story spread across the globe, causing many to step forward and support him ranging from comedians Ricky Gervais and Jonathan Pie, up through yours truly, who prior to the trial live streamed for eight hours, helping raise over $20,000 for his defense. Meecham, despite his conviction has refused to pay his fine, stating that he'd rather go to prison on principle than pay his way out of a conviction he should have never been tried for in the first place.

To think though, that an arrest and court case such as that which played out in Scotland could not only garner international attention, but do so as the result of what was in fact a harmless YouTube video and prank, says a great deal about what the modern sensitivity culture which has cropped up in recent years really means for free expression. In the same way that the court jester is regarded as the only member of the court who can speak truth to power without the same worry of consequences as all others, it is important for us all to recognize that without comedic freedom, the freedom to mock, deride, lampoon, satirize and just generally laugh about anything we choose, our fundamental right to speak freely at all is itself put in grave jeopardy.

THE VALUE OF WRITING

Christopher Hitchens, the late great atheist firebrand and contrarian, famously once told an audience of university students that should they have a desire to be writers, that college was unnecessary. Stating that for one to be able to write, all they needed to be able to do was speak and then crushing a number of students by asking how many could say others were openly excited to hear them when they did, Hitchens' own style of writing and speech was one which relied as much on his confidence with his words as they did his exquisite mastery of the language itself. Bold to the point of brash, it was by way of his numerous talks, speeches, debates, readings and books that the former Vanity Fair columnist became not only famous, but immortalized as one of the great thinkers of the 20th century.

In much the same way Hitchens praised and celebrated the works, life and ideas of his predecessors such as Spinoza, Payne and Orwell, newer generations of writers and intellectuals have taken to remembering and vaunting the inspiration they found in him as they seek to tackle our modern issues. Though existing in different overall environments, the questions and contentions of today are much the same as they've always been in respect to matters such as cultural politics, the conflicts between secularism and religious dominionism, and of course free expression. Yet in much the same way that many who seek to invoke the names and legends of America's "founding fathers" often misread, misinterpret or misrepresent the thoughts and writings of these men now long dead, so too have many taken to Hitchens and his works in a very similar fashion.

To begin with, in respect to the modern free speech battle, many on what I've taken to calling the 'soft right,' – meaning those who routinely adopt and promote conservative ideals while promoting themselves as ostensibly liberal — have come to often elevate and revere Hitchens for his ardent support for free speech, especially in respect to matters of blasphemy laws and outrage culture. To be certain in this respect that Hitchens was what we now generally refer to as a free speech absolutist, there can be no doubts as to his dedication to such a cause. However often in their attempts to further vaunt the works, words and legacy of this iconic writer, many tend it seems to project a great deal more of their own ideology onto his memory than his conventionally promoted stances would seem to warrant.

Just as quickly as many on the "save the west" free speech side of the argument are to invoke the name of Hitchens and quotes such as *"If someone tells me that I've hurt their feelings, I say, 'I'm still waiting to hear what your point is. In this country, I've been told, 'That's offensive' as if those two words constitute an argument or a comment. Not to me they don't. And I'm not running for anything, so I don't have to pretend to like people when I don't,"* they quite often also tend to conflate his positions against Islam and outrage culture with being aligned with them in respect to other matters, such as economics and socio-economics. Railing endlessly against what can easily be regarded as a new 'red menace,' which purports to be combatting "neo-Marxism" and "Trotskist entryism" which are promoted as being real and present threats creeping into and throughout every aspect of western civilization, many who know Hitchens primarily through YouTube videos of his talks, as opposed to his substantial body of written works, tend to overlook at Hitchens himself came proudly from a "hard left," and "Trotskist" position.

However these sorts of contradictions, as common as they are within these new fledgling activists and online activist movements, are not themselves the underlying point, but rather mere elements to the overall matter of what lasts and what doesn't in respect to popular thought. Every modern generation has its celebrity pundit class. From talk radio and cable news, up through web based news and talk programs, the evolution and existence of the "talking head" is quite often sadly emblematic of the pop-culture politics of a given age. With 'hot takes' and 'run downs' often being used in lieu of more robust and in depth analyses of matters, it tends to fall, as it has throughout history, to the writers of a time to properly encapsulate the ideas and realities which cannot be adequately summed up in a tweet, tee-shirt of thirty second sound byte.

In truth, even as the proliferation of digital media, information and communications technology and the overall news cycle itself continue to each respectively double in scope and speed with each passing year, the value and raw necessity of the written word has not only been sustained amidst this ever-changing media landscape, but has in fact increased as rising numbers of bloggers, vloggers, content creators and hot take originators continue to dominate popular conversations. Whereas in the past, a debate was generally regarded more like an orderly court case than a flat out argument, in our modern era, shouting matches and reciprocated volleys of slogan and buzz-word exchanges have come to overtake this concept.

Likewise, whereas in the past, one was encouraged to slowly read and consider the thoughts of an intellectual, it is now far more common for those of enthusiastic political convictions to simply take up a headline or snappy retort and then repeat such ad-nauseum as a means to promote a particular view. However long before and still resting beneath this abysmal imposter for intelligent discourse, the written word allowed sound or even simply logical concepts to be deeply enshrined in public thought in ways that modern trends and attention grabbers simply fail to do, despite volume and regularity.

A major piece to this reality is reflected in the simple matter of time. The time it takes for an author to fully flesh out the ideas they wish to express. The time is takes for a reader to mentally ingest and consider that which is on offer. In both cases, rather than merely digesting a spoken phrase or printed headline, the writer is obligated to ensure their words are as true as they can be, while at the same time the reader is challenged to dwell a bit longer upon that which is presented and truly think about what is being expressed. Just as Ben Shapiro shot to fame repeating his now infamous line "facts don't care about your feelings," within the context of honest literature, both Shapiro and his readers are (or at least ought to be) forced to linger on the questions of which facts, how factual they are as well as which feelings and why they're being felt. This is fundamentally where both the disconnect between the written word and conventional media arise, as well as where the indispensable value of the latter is best observed.

For an analogy to further illustrate this point, let me first reflect upon an older lesson from a different medium. Prior to my work as a writer (that meaning before I took my writing on professionally) I was myself trained as a screen actor. Having never worked on stage, my training and ambition was to work for film. While studying under the tutelage of actors Chris Berry, Dean West and Daniel Dupont, I would often reflect upon the nervous fear which kept me from the stage.

The notion was a simple one. On screen, one can have as many takes as is required to get the scene right before moving onto the next. This contrasted with the stage, where after rehearsals, there was but one chance per show to get the scenes right and any flub or mistake made in the course of such, was immediate to all in attendance. My thinking at the time being that between the two mediums of film and stage, stage was such where a fuck up was simply unforgivable.

However in the course of my education as an actor, each of my teachers pointed out a single and easily overlooked reality. That being that no matter how perfect or imperfect a performance on screen might be, it was forever. This in contrast to the stage, wherein should a line be dropped or a scene disrupted in one performance, such could be avoided in the future.

"How many actors can you think of who've been panned for life over a botched stage play?" Berry would ask, following up with, "now how many actors who've fucked up in a movie never lived it down?"

In this simple lesson, a small universe of creative realities expanded before my eyes, following me to this very day. Short of some viral clip online, how many notable authors have been forever lambasted or praised over slips of the tongue or simple hot takes, versus those whose written words, standing as emblems of their thoughts and beliefs, have wrought the same? To be certain, the numbers skew in obvious directions given the overall varied and lasting nature of statements, thought of and expressed in these various manners.

Just as the production of a film requires repeated filming of certain scenes so as to get them just right, so too does the crafting of the written word require greater forethought and direction than do the buzzword laden news and media appearances of public intellectuals of our modern time. Just as in the course of filming a scene for a movie, a director, writer or actor may have reason to pause and reflect upon that being expressed and in the course of such, refine or reform that on the page. So too then do the writers of books or longer form articles and essays find the same opportunity to reflect upon the ideas on offer and dwell just a bit longer upon them to shore up any logical, factual or philosophical inconsistencies they may encounter.

Yet beneath this central matter of import in respect to the crafting of the written word, the fundamental reality of both its lasting impact and the process of its thesis adoption or rejection by the reader remains itself central to its value. In a fashion that obligates a thinker to firstly and most hopefully suspend assumption of fact or claim one way or another and to in turn, dwell slightly longer than they might were the words and concepts on offer to be delivered more rhetorically, the determination of value in regards to ideas and statements is allowed to take on a fuller and more robust life of its own. In the same way that the writer themselves is obligated to pour greater amounts of thought into both concept and presentation than is required in general discussion, so too does the audience of said piece, through the simple action of sitting quietly and reading it, ideally find opportunity to delve deeper into the notions and concepts presented.

In both of these, now heavily labored respects, the indispensible value of the written word as both when written and finally read, largely lies with the obligated egress from clamor and the retreat into thoughtful isolation. Through elimination of committee in both crafting and receiving of expression, through the shuttering of the corridors of personal or intellectual influence and through the embrace of quiet curiosity, the inalienable worth to our second oldest form of record can no more be denied than it can be properly stymied by the ever growing cacophony of flashy new media. Across the globe and the expanses of time itself, the significance of written expression is one forged at both ends of the expressive pipeline, wrought most observably in isolation and quiet.

THE ISOLATION OF WRITING

Whether one seeks to expound and elaborate upon matters of life, society, faith or politics in direct prose, or wishes to derive from their imagination tales of fiction and fantasy, a central and inescapable factor to this effort in writing is that of solitude. Granted, the history of writers and their works are littered with tales and anecdotes of writers penning articles, chapters and books in bar rooms or other public spaces. However even within these histories themselves, within the mind of the working writer a defined focus is required that can function like blinders on a horse.

Unlike the work of so many other artists, writing is a singularly solitary profession. While indeed great numbers of writers collaborate with others in the course of their writing, be it for research or actual writing partnerships, the act itself is one of isolation. Whereas musicians, actors or even visual artists can and often are required to engage with others in the course of their creative processes, the cerebral nature of writing is one which draws the creator generally deep into the recesses of their own mind.

This is not to say that influence is not an issue though, by far. In point of fact, it is in many ways a more pressing and troublesome matter for the writer than it is for many in the other aforementioned mediums. In much the same way that a guitarist who spends two days listening to Metallica might find themselves inadvertently or unintentionally lifting from the styling of Kirk Hammett, through the simple act of indulging in the written or spoken words of a favorite author, writers can very often fall into the unfortunate habit of borrowing a voice when they hadn't intended to. So much so, many writers, myself included, tend to avoid reading or oratory while in the process of crafting a longer form work.

Within the descriptive, prescriptive and proscriptive elements of crafting a work from first draft to final edit, everything from one's specific style and usage of the language, to the actual substance of the piece are such that be it physically, or merely mentally, a good writer is obligated to remove themselves from the world and the world from themselves in pursuit of completing their copy. When considered in the vein of the political, philosophical or conceptual, this self-imposed exile or isolation carries an even greater weight than merely allowing for the peace to think and write in clear terms, but allows for a processing of concepts that is free from the distraction of chattering classes. Unrestrained by such a writer can even find in merely the course of attempting to illustrate or define a topic, ground shaking revelations that might be otherwise impossible to realize with prattling masses still in ear shot.

Here yet another example of the inherent value to quiet and stillness in regards to thought can be observed, perhaps in its purest distillation. Much as with philosophers of old, quiet contemplation preceding revelation of new or defined thought allows for such to be more thoroughly fleshed out, if not merely better articulated. To take time in the consideration of not only a point one enjoys or cares for, but its framing and presentation serves in this respect as something of an initial proving ground for ideas. In the same way a great idea is meaningless without the words or deeds to define it, the process of doing such begs a second, third or fourth consideration, if not outright dashing it to pieces as it proceeds to be unpacked. However this essential quality to the work of writing is not limited simply to the needed quiet for production itself. In much the same way that freedom from distraction can enable the necessary focus required to get the writing done, the elimination of outside influence and suggestion is likewise crucial for the drafting of concept and idea itself.

Imagine that you were attempting to balance a checkbook or ledger. Dozens of entries adding and subtracting values of different sorts, populate a spreadsheet that you must tally line by line. Now imagine attempting to do this in a busy transit station, with everything from the roaring of buses or trains, down to announcements over a PA system and a homeless person muttering random strings of inconsequential numbers right beside you. As difficult as that may sound, it rather accurately describes the challenges of influence many writers face when sat down at their desk, even when surrounded by actual and sustained silence.

As is the case with most any conceivable art form, a great deal of the personal value one can find in it comes not even in the pride of a finished product, as much as in the process of the craft itself. Much in the way as how the art which we consume can allow us to escape or transcend the daily doldrums of life and society, the isolated creation of such likewise offers the writer both a chance to step away from the noise of the world, while also in many instances, a calm and measured means by which to consider it. The turning of a phrase or crafting of a sentence in this capacity, refining the very thought itself through the simple necessity of paying slightly more regard to how it is expressed.

PESSIMISM

In the most honest sense I can offer it to you dear reader, we as a species and society are hopelessly and irrevocably fucked. In the same manner one could and perhaps ought to view the progression of mankind from our primitive roots to our ostensibly advanced and enlightened state of being as evidence that we are on what one could consider an upward trajectory, we must at the same time observe and consider how little actually seems to change. Though our wars may not be fought in the open name of empire or conquest, the functional motivations for them more often than not rest with a convoluted representation of such, with modern nationalistic or religious propagandizing simply utilizing new tools to invoke old sentiments.

Likewise so many a domestic or internal matter of strife proves to invoke modernized reinterpretations of antiquated excuses for the existence of things such as poverty, addiction, crime, graft and corruption. Ranging from the Calvinist approaches which deem that god, or perhaps just the assigned or assumed lot in life is what leads people to ruin, up through more ideological orthodoxies insisting that all plights a society faces stems from its inability or refusal to adopt wholesale whatever precepts or assumed solutions the ideologue holds, the numerous excuses created for the miseries and plights are quite often, when held in comparison to those of old, merely polished and refined explanations or justifications for matters which have plagued mankind since its beginnings. Though one could go as far as saying either that such matters themselves are either inevitable and wholly natural to us, or nothing like they used to be and merely new issues requiring new, as of yet un-established methods of redress, the ultimate reality at the end of the day is that they persist regardless.

Though some modern thinkers who would wish to shed light on such often make mention of our basic nature as being just slightly more complex primates than our biological ancestors, with still under-developed frontal lobes and a most unfortunate tendency for credulity, reflections of a deeper philosophical pessimism seem to be as readily available even without our pop-culture and entertainment as they do in the writings of French or German absurdist and nihilist philosophers. In the HBO series "True Detective," the character of Rust Cohle, played by Matthew McConaughey famously expounds upon a general concept of philosophical pessimism in one (of many) scenes, stating:

"I think human consciousness is a tragic misstep in evolution. We became too self-aware. Nature created an aspect of nature separate from itself. We are creatures that should not exist by natural law. We are things that labor under the illusion of having a self, this accretion of sensory experience and feelings, programmed with total assurance that we are each somebody, when in fact everybody's nobody. I think the honorable thing for our species to do is to deny our programming. Stop reproducing. Walk hand in

hand into extinction. One last midnight, brothers and sisters opting out of a raw deal."

Within this somewhat nihilist, somewhat absurdist and genuinely pessimistic quote, the fundamental question of humanity's species-wide sense of individualism and meaning, strikes rather centrally to the deeper questions of free will, which in turn require the consideration as to whether or not everything from our ostensible progression as a species, down to the perpetual plights and difficulties we face in turn, are less a matter of will or collective choice and more one of an unwilling following of our naturalistic programming as biological machines. This in and of itself on a philosophical level could be viewed as somewhat dismaying, yet an added layer of pessimistic interpretation can even be afforded to us by the simple fact that in this 21st western century, where information and the intellectual legacies of history's great thinkers are on perpetual offer freely, with just a keystroke on the internet required to retrieve them, that it requires a fictional television show and the presence of a movie star, simply to introduce so many to the concepts and questions themselves.

To wonder then if the underlying nature and reality to our time here on Earth as supposedly sentient individuals who may or may not be simply suffering under a perception based delusion of such, as well as a society comprised of people operating under the similar delusion that change and progress comes from will and effort, is not ultimately just one enormous scripted story, playing itself out according to deeper nature realities we're simply unable or unwilling to accept becomes somewhat unavoidable. The classic apathetic shrug which presumes in a fatalistic sentiment that all that is, is and that all which will be shall be becomes a resignation to some biologically pre-ordained fate and the surrender of will, or the concept of will, happens as par for course. Yet in a strange way, a certain type of liberation is found, or can be found, as this concept settles in the mind as a final reality.

In much the same way a nihilist who still smiles can expound on the absence of objective meaning to life, giving way to the embracing of a subjective sense of such and thereby making it their own, this fatalistic pessimism can serve the purpose of alleviating the sorts of stresses and strains that the concepts of optimism meeting abject failure can bring about. What reason is there to worry at all if the problems of our age neither have any actual solutions or are solvable at all? In a somewhat famous quote from the Dalai Llama on the topic of worry, he said *"If a problem can be fixed, there is no need to worry. If it cannot be fixed, worrying will do no good."*

Though certainly not a pessimist or nihilist himself in any genuine or even interpreted sense of the word, this very notion of concern being a waste of time and energy in respect to the perils and plights we face as a species and society rings just as true when the pessimistic perspective is adopted. Given that as a species which seeks to be *–or at least present itself as seeking to be-* divorced from its naturalistic roots, separate and distinct from other forms of life by virtue either of our evolutionary intellect, or our "souls," as the faithful often wish to insist upon, the adoption of the absurdist perspective which states that the human condition is one that is inherently mismatched between our desires and our reality can be seen as liberating when the unpleasant truth of the philosophy is accepted.

But take it a step further if you're so daring. Consider what would have happened if anything had been different throughout the course of your life. What would be, had you known then what you know now. Take the consideration into the palm of your hand and look at it, in its entirety.

Were you not forced by your nature, as opposed to your choice, to be where you are now, than how much of what you have would you dream of giving up entirely for the dice roll's chance of something better? Would the loves you've had and lost been better to have never been at all and would those you love you now not be worth holding to yourself as you do now, on the offer that such could be otherwise different entirely? If everything that matters to you now is to be seen as a part of what you are and is to mean anything at all, does it mean anything at all if it's more a product of something beyond yourself, outside of your choice or will and as you might say "simply" a matter of how it ended up being, than it would be had you chosen it with the clarity of foreknowledge?

But perhaps these waffling philosophical questions of pessimism are a bit beyond the pale in relation to what we consider to be the broader issues we tend to face on a societal scale. So to bring it back to a conventional question; is the dour run of the mill pessimism, that of the hopeless and doomed perspective which says that everything is terrible and will only get worse, actually an altogether harmful thing unto itself? Certainly a life lived according to the precept that nothing will ever work out and that the mysteries of tomorrow should be viewed with suspicion, caution and a presumption of failure is one which on a personal level is bound to cause undue stress and anxiety. But is it inherently bad on a level making it useless?

To "prepare for the worst and hope for the best" is undoubtedly a fine perspective for the "survivor." To take as it sets manageable expectations which on their worst days are simply affirmed, while on their betters surpassed, it is an exceptionally safe and altogether sensible ethos on which to operate. In this particular sense one could almost claim that pessimism of this sort is simply optimism for realists. Yet just as it can be easy to view the progression from brutal Bronze Age savagery to advanced, interconnected economies of information and communication as wholly beneficial, the perilous tradeoffs made along the way often go unnoticed until they're too late.

Just as the darker sides to things such as social media have exposed the uglier sides to human behavior, making the boorish and cheap into goldmines for those whose very boorish and cheap behaviors earns them the esteemed and unfortunate title of "influencers," the horrors of our exponential advances in technology and complexity only seem to make themselves apparent once it's too late to really do anything about it. Though we may not spill foreign blood in the names of gods or empires as we once did, we now instead do so with a clinical and mechanical efficiency which relies on intricate mechanisms of public persuasion. Whereas we are now able to produce goods at rates and volumes unimaginable to previous generations, the goods themselves have largely lost all sense of craft or value, making the necessary disposable and replaceable rather than invaluable and repairable.

This onward slog into a future which is increasingly brightened only by the flashing LEDs of commercial excitement is one which has, as numerous studies have shown over time, brought consistently equal if not deeper levels of stress and dismay that lie often beneath the glossy promises of a consistently better tomorrow. As tomorrow then becomes today, we lament lacking the foresight to have seen these problems coming as we note our political divisions, our social hostilities, our stresses over either not having enough to live or following this, not having enough to live "happily" and the ever-present evolution of newer and more insidious threats to our lives, happiness and safety announced to us by way of an unending stream of news, gossip and information all in their own rights and often in conjunction with each other, getting worse as time goes on.

If one were to argue that the world is not the problem, but our perception of it, then we who make the world what it is are the root cause of our woes. If we are to take that in reverse and assume that a worsening state of affairs is, in spite of things such as longer lifespans and broadening economic security, a real intangible progression, than we remain as doomed as we are in the former scenario. This inescapable pessimism however, which observes cause and effect to bring about twice the plight as it does improvement, is not without its own inherent virtue.

In much the way it would take a complete fool to attempt a climb on Mt. Everest with little more than a pair of boots and water bottle, a managed pessimism can and I would personally say should be embraced as a call for preparation and careful thinking. Whether it be the stubborn voice of a doom-sayer in conversation with others or simply a nagging voice in the folds of one's own mind and thoughts, the presumption of failure is both one which can help us avoid pitfalls down the line at best and provide a buffer from the wretched sting of failure should and when such come to pass. It could rightfully be argued that the very nature of bureaucracy (*a term which itself is in some ways unjustly loaded with presumptions of corruption and inefficiency*) is one which serves this very necessary pessimistic function in the business of government.

Much as common partisan banter routinely warns a party in power that the accumulation of centralized authority will inevitably present that power to their adversaries when the 'pendulum' swings back once again, the effective purpose of bureaucracy in systems of government is one that is meant to stymie or hinder the advancing of radical agendas which themselves often put ideals over functional practicality. The creation and maintaining of systems which are meant to check, double check, triple check, then approve, return for review and revision, re-check, table, reconsider, revisit, reform, reintroduce, negotiate, table again, revive again, reform again, debate again, approve, re-approve and then perhaps do nothing at all with a proposed program, policy or idea, though bothersome, can very easily be argued to be essential in the securing of safe and stable progress. Though to frame it in such a way is almost satirical at a first glance, this "small c" conservative approach to matters can be viewed as altogether essential when thought upon without the biases set upon it by general or popular regard.

As with seemingly all things related to our imperfect social structures, wrought of imperfect human thought and desire and our perpetually imperfect attempts to make sense of it all, pessimism, both in philosophy and common practice is something which must be embraced and understood, as well as carefully managed and balanced in accordance with its counterpart. Too much and nothing will ever change, happen or get better. Too little and we will find ourselves barreling headlong into one disaster after another. As with all things, the nature to pessimism relies on balance and honest consideration.

A HAPPY SENSE OF NOTHING

One of perhaps the greatest sources for human suffering tends to spring from our innate desire for there to be meaning in our lives. We are naturally pattern seeking creatures, who expect if not demand to find order, structure and meaning even where there is none. Beyond this, given the strains of our still as-of-yet misunderstood egos and senses of self, we often tend also to seek these points of order and meaning in a manner that pertains to, if not centers entirely on ourselves.

It is often said by atheists in debates with believers, that one of the observably silliest parts of religion is its tendency to ascribe the existence of the universe itself to the will of god as it relates to the existence of man. "God gave us this Earth," and so on being common refrains, asserting in essence that the purpose of our planet and everything upon it is here specifically *for us* as opposed to the naturalistic understanding that we, like all other things upon it, living or dead in fact grew from it and not the other way around. While this view on the part of the faithful can be dismissed as a form of near solipsistic egocentrism, the naturally occurring desire which lies beneath it to find objective order and meaning in a universe which we are increasingly observing to have little in the way of such is both observable and understandable.

It is however also an entirely futile exercise. Not merely because this search will result in either failure or a contrived false positive wrought from the stubborn desire for such to be the case, but also in that with every step one takes in such a direction, they set themselves up for either a sustained delusion or abject and sometimes crushing existential failure. You can call it nihilism, you can call it absurdism, you can even call it naturalism, but just as the argument goes from the perspective of a creationist that the complex and intricate systems of everything in the universe operate so perfectly that they must be the work of a creator, the answer from the skeptical epistemic is invariably that it has to work just so as if it didn't, one would not be around to question its nature at all.

Yet within so many minds the very concept of the universe as a whole being a cold and uncaring, ultimately "meaningless" place with no genuine rhyme or reason as to why things happen, or genuine objective purpose to any of it, is one which can send shivers down ones spine and stir within us senses of dread and despondency. Why though? Is it not better to confront an uncomfortable truth for what it is than to perpetually chase a manifest fantasy simply for the sake of *feeling* better about things?

While a common defense of religion is that it offers hope to the hopeless, it could easily be said that such is a false hope, promising a reward after death of a brighter and happier existence than perhaps they have in life when there is nothing more than the words of old books to suggest such at all. While perhaps it may raise the spirits of an individual, it does little to address either the plights they may be lamenting, or give them any genuine grounded sense as to how to grasp on to whatever Earthly or corporeal aspects of their life they may have cause to embrace. It is in this sense, an existential sugar pill. A placebo, offered in lieu of some more proper medication or salve to help bring about a more robust philosophical or intellectual relief by way of an even slightly more sophisticated understanding of life in the universe.

So why then meaninglessness? How does absurdism or nihilistic rejection of even the notion of objective meaning help in this regard? To those who insist that there is such, the common question of the apparent numinous nature to love is often brought up. Though sometimes pithy in its own right, the believer will ask one to explain the concept and experience of love and present that as evidence as to the existence of something ethereal and meaningful. Yet in counter to this, even if one is to break down the concept of love to it merely being a natural mechanism by which the perpetuation of species might occur, the relative beauty is almost best observed so long as one has released their sense of import in regards to themselves and their place in the scheme of things. This being in that for anyone who has been in love or felt love or felt as though they were loved, the impression and personal emotional impact of such is impossible to deny. But does this make it an objective experience or subjective? Does that lofty sensation in the midst of it, or the powerful throes we experience when it's gone exist outside of ourselves in some broader, esoteric manner?

I think not. And furthermore, I would say that if it did, then it would rather sully the whole affair. This being because such should exist as something exclusively within ourselves, something wrought of our own nature, even as a matter of raw mechanical biological function, it means that we own the experience entirely. No longer sharing it with gods or spirits or some external purpose, it becomes and is allowed to exist as something wholly personal and by extension, all the more powerful. So such is likewise true in relation to broader concepts of value and meaning.

Regardless of what you might like to call it, the act of abandoning a search for objective meaning in life and the replacing of it with a search simply for subjective meaning is itself a wholly liberating experience. To be sure, it is not without its own pitfalls or dangers as to dive down the existential rabbit hole of meaninglessness in this way can and often does lead the unready traveler to some exceptionally dark places. But just as the abandoning of rigid ideology or absolutist philosophy frees a mind, allowing it to consider questions or issues from more dynamic perspectives, so too does the abandoning of a fruitless search for more fundamental existential meaning liberate one in a manner that allows them to better claim true ownership of their thoughts, feelings, values and sense of self.

For an example, which would you likely find more altogether impressive? The sentience, self-awareness, wonder and awe that the sentient and self-aware human being experiences being merely the work of a craftsman who simply designed us to be this way, or alternately, the totality of our ability to think, live and experience the world being the result of a fantastic natural evolution, from which the attributes and advances we've enjoyed as a species sprang naturally into existence. On the one hand, to claim for example that a creator, who would undoubtedly need to be all powerful or at least, powerful to a degree we cannot adequately comprehend without the aid of fantasy literature, would state that the vivacious nature to the human experience was as much a simple feature to our design, much as cup holder might be in a late nineties sedan.

Alternately however if, as the philosophical pessimist might suggest, this intellect, self-awareness and overall sense of self is more a byproduct of our natural development which, as we can observe on a naturalistic level, often operates contrary to what might otherwise fit in correctly with the natural world around us, it stands out as something wholly remarkable. An element of nature which exists to one degree or another outside of or parallel to it, with the rest of physical world following presumably sensible functions that we in this case, are able to both observe and consider. Rather than merely being an added feature in this case, gifted unto us by some external force with an actual purpose for it being so, it becomes instead something that is entirely our own and that we in the course of experiencing are left to ponder and explore it for what it is, rather than what we'd like it to be.

This all naturally must sound horridly nebulous really and that is not without reason. In much the same manner that one will find the initial introduction to the philosophical questions of self and self-awareness mind bogglingly complex, perhaps around adolescence as they begin more fully developing a sense of personal identity or later upon their first reading of Søren Kierkegaard, grappling with the notion that only meaning in one's life is that of the subjective can be an exceptionally tricky endeavor unto itself. If life is without objective concrete meaning, does that not mean that life itself is pointless?

Once again, as it is a matter of subjective opinion, the answer is "sort of." For a thought experiment in this regard, consider an asteroid on a collision course with the Earth. For millennia this large hunk of rock, metal and ice has hurtled through open space under the direction only of various sources of gravity and its own undying momentum. At long last its course has brought it barreling towards the Earth where it will collide with the pale blue dot wiping out all traces of life. From the perspective of life on Earth, this is an altogether bad thing. From the perspective of the asteroid, it means ultimately nothing at all save for that its long journey is coming to an end.

When the doom finally arrives, the Earth is cracked and destroyed and everyone and everything on it dies. Before they die, many lament that they'll not have the chance to hug their loved ones, witness beauty, enjoy a sandwich and so on, ever again, but then they're gone. The universe itself continues on about its own business without missing a tick. Were those lives lost meaningless?

Well certainly to the universe as a whole and most definitely to the asteroid which snuffed them all out. But just before they died, the creatures who lived those lives largely tended to value them. There was nothing outside of their own sense of value in play there, as no divine intervention stopped them from being wiped out, but in their time they found, or at least sought and sensed a value and meaning. Now if the three players in this instance being the asteroid, the universe and the life on Earth shared a ratio of only one-third of involved parties giving the slightest damn about life itself with the other two objectively having no care or concern about anything at all, the totality of value and meaning comes solely from its own source. In this, objectively speaking while life is proven to be ultimately irrelevant to the physical universe itself, it nevertheless remains wholly and entirely relevant to the living parties themselves. Therefore, we can say with some certainty that if nothing else, life "sort of" matters.

But staying with this just a bit longer, if the totality of value or meaning of life comes exclusively from the relative perspective of the living, this means that essentially that relative perspective, existing as the only posited perspective on offer sets the bar as to what value or meaning exists at all. Though this may sound as though it is merely a roundabout way of saying "nothing means anything," it in fact suggests, if not demands that the reins in this case stay wholly in the hands of the rider and not be given up under any circumstances. In this, it curiously enough insists that in our considerations, that the meaning not be 'found' in life, but derived from it.

Beauty, majesty, the awe inspiring...these come not from without, but are reflected upon within. A sunset is merely the sight of the celestial bodies continuing their millenniums long dance in the vacuum of space, but to see one, especially a striking one in perhaps the late spring or early summer, is something which many if not most of us find entrancing no matter how regular it may be. The rush and thrill of looking deep into a lovers eyes and sharing a sense of passionate connection, is more likely than not nothing more than psycho-social reflexes born of biological determinism. But that doesn't make the experience any less enthralling, even when one recognizes that it may be nothing but hormones and endorphins.

In fact it can be argued, as it is in the context of this essay, that experiencing beauty, love and majesty of the likes people tend to like to ascribe something "higher" than or "beyond" ourselves is actually enhanced as an experience when we allow the feelings and impressions of them to be our own entirely. To retain or reclaim ownership of such feelings and thoughts while abandoning the desire for them to exist separate from ourselves in some way, allows not only for us to own them and hold them even closer to our being, but in the course of such, allows for an even more personal sense of what it is to be human or alive at all. In this sense, as strange as it may seem to consider, we can in our throwing off of demands for deeper meaning, find such residing within ourselves, reliant only upon our willingness to accept it raw and purely wherever and whenever we find it.

THE SOLUTION IS PEOPLE

Realistically, given that there is no god, no objective meaning or purpose to our existence and that it is entirely unlikely that a benevolent and enlightened alien species will touch down and show us the way, the only viable source for genuine solutions to the problems which we face or means by which to derive purpose and meaning at all, is us. People. Human beings who, either collectively en masse calm down to craft real and actionable fixes, or by simple virtue of reaching some critical cataclysm wherein we're forced by the pressing weight of raw and indisputable circumstance, manage to understand and tame the impulses and instincts which drive us into the numerous ditches we find ourselves in.

Though you'd be right to call it "pie in the sky" thinking, the first step to undoing the mad dash towards the insipid oblivion which we've collectively set ourselves to is for people in general to slow down. Not merely to offer deeper considerations of the matters at hand, but also to allow themselves the sorts of managed distractions that can allow their mental cache to clear. As one matter piles atop another, as one breaking news story or heated public debate overtakes and melts into the last, the all-or-nothing mad-dash mentality that such patterns create within people can often serve to overtake their reason and critical faculties even faster than whatever ideological or philosophical convictions they may hold might serve to guide them to an answer.

Were they, were *we* to slow down and realize that though news cycles have become untamed beasts unto themselves, that it rests with the people, both individually and in groups, to parse out fact from fiction and meaning from bullshit, the sorts of nonsense which unfortunately makes up the fuel for the bitter and pedantic shouting matches which equate modern debate would be hamstrung and powerless. Were we to somehow remember the bygone days when to see past the spin and manipulation of media outlets, that we need not simply to gravitate routinely to those we prefer or those which reaffirm what we prefer to be "true," but quietly absorb and consider as objectively as we can, all sources of information and weigh their respective validity against one another, parsing out the truth from the lies. Were we to take these simple first steps, we would find the power of the vacuous and voracious demagoguery which presently dominates our conversations would be diminished.

Though it can be easy with the panicky nonsense and derisive hostility which seems to dominate seemingly every aspect of public life, it is important to remember that within each of us is the capacity to be sane, reasonable and though we may not agree, congenial to one another. It will of course be quite the challenge to assume this as the standard and consistent mindset, especially at the rates with which news stories assault us and the combative opinions on our social media feeds, in our workplaces and perhaps even at our dinner tables tend to follow suit, but even then if the simple act of recognizing the counterproductive nature of such can become a matter of habit, an effort to restore calm mindfulness can more effectively be taken. To be certain, flightiness, hostility, reactionary impulses will be forever a part of our basic psychological and intellectual makeup and to be certain, there will likely be no chance of ever fully ridding ourselves as such.

But just as so many inspirational figures throughout the history of our species have shown us, people tend to greatly admire and often wish to emulate the sorts of peace, poise and reasonableness which comes with managed temperament. Even when figures such as Ghandi, Mandela or Lincoln are found through deeper research to be as flawed as anyone else, holding ideas or perhaps carrying out acts which stand in stark contrast to iconography of their legends, it is this unease with which we note these failings that speaks to a deeper desire to strive for egalitarian humanism and a sense of enlightenment. As cliché as it may be to say, it is less the destination than the journey in this sense, as in a universe which we generally know to be anything but static, the closest any of us can ever hope to attaining any real form of perfection is the constant onward striving for such, no matter how unattainable it may be.

There are those who in apathy and resignation will point out that violence, predation, graft, hatred, malevolence, war, poverty and misery have always and likely will always beset us as civilizations no matter what we do. Yet it has been through our generally ceaseless efforts to address these as we can, to derive newer and newer solutions to old problems that we've gone from simple hominids learning by trial and error that which we can and cannot eat off the forest floor, to slightly more advanced hominids tweaking the genes of the foods we prefer to ensure they can last longer in our grocery stores and in our pantries. With cautious optimism, a tempered pessimism, a determination not to be fooled and the fortitude to admit to ourselves when we have been, with patience for those whose ideals we find repulsive and an inquisitive skepticism for those with whom we agree and most of all, with a routine dedication to a regular examination and re-examination of everything we think that we know and how it squares with everything new which we learn, the perpetual cycles of noise, nonsense and credulous stupidity which hamper us from making real headway on the matters and issues we face can at the very least, be mitigated in the course of the deliberations which follow.

Human duality rests perhaps as an absurdity at our core and it indeed and without question is a stumbling block built firmly into our minds which is bound to trip us up. However not all that is in conflict in such a way ought necessarily be viewed through the myopic lens of hopeless intractability. In the same fashion that the illogical and often destructive emotion of love itself can drive us mad as it conflicts with objective truths and nature we live with, it's shining underlying romanticism and overall place in the pantheon of human motivations can easily suggest that such inherent duality is as often complimentary as it is divisive.

This is not a hope or faith that such may come to pass, as hope is the last bastion of the doomed and faith, the last bastion of the fool. But rather it is an insistence that the capacity of reason and ambition to evolve resides within every sane human being. Perhaps even, in those such as writers and philosophers whose sanity is so often found to be in question.

ACKNOWLEDGMENTS

Christoph, for giving me the chance to do what I'd always dreamed of doing.

Leza, for her tireless scrutiny of my generally sloppy prose.

Justin Little, a dear friend who I'm proud to know history will regard me as a contemporary of.

To those of brighter minds than mine for lighting the way, to those of duller mindsets for demonstrating what a fool can look like and finally to those who follow them, proving once and for all who the bigger fool between the two truly is.

ABOUT THE AUTHOR

Nicholas Goroff is a writer, host, content creator and actor. He has played principle or leading roles in over fourteen films, published hundreds of articles as a beer, cocktail and travel critic and been viewed over a million times on YouTube. Prior to this he worked for a decade as a political contractor in the professional PAC, union and activism worlds, and wrote extensively for subversive political journals such as Occupy and The Rationalists.

ALSO BY CLASH BOOKS

TRAGEDY QUEENS: STORIES INSPIRED BY LANA DEL REY & SYLVIA PLATH
Edited by Leza Cantoral

GIRL LIKE A BOMB
Autumn Christian

CENOTE CITY
Monique Quintana

99 POEMS TO CURE WHATEVER'S WRONG WITH YOU OR CREATE THE PROBLEMS YOU NEED
Sam Pink

THIS BOOK IS BROUGHT TO YOU BY MY STUDENT LOANS
Megan J. Kaleita

THE MISADVENTURES OF A JILTED JOURNALIST
Justin Little

HEXIS
Charlene Elsby

ARSENAL/SIN DOCUMENTOS

Francesco Levato

FOGHORN LEGHORN

Big Bruiser Dope Boy

TRY NOT TO THINK BAD THOUGHTS

Art by Matthew Revert

SEQUELLAND

Jay Slayton-Joslin

JAH HILLS

Unathi Slasha

NEW VERONIA

M.S. Coe

THE HAUNTING OF THE PARANORMAL ROMANCE AWARDS

Christoph Paul & Mandy De Sandra

DARK MOONS RISING IN A STARLESS NIGHT

Mame Bougouma Diene

TRASH PANDA

Leza Cantoral

GODLESS HEATHENS: CONVERSATIONS WITH ATHEISTS

Edited by Andrew J. Rausch

WE PUT THE LIT IN LITERARY
CLASHBOOKS.COM
FOLLOW US ON TWITTER, IG & FB @clashbooks

EMAIL US
clashmediabooks@gmail.com

www.ingramcontent.com/pod-product-compliance
Lightning Source LLC
Chambersburg PA
CBHW030118100526
44591CB00009B/442